Quoting Corinthians

Quoting Corinthians

IDENTIFYING SLOGANS AND
QUOTATIONS IN 1 CORINTHIANS

Edward W. Watson
Martin M. Culy

☙PICKWICK *Publications* • Eugene, Oregon

QUOTING CORINTHIANS
Identifying Slogans and Quotations in 1 Corinthians

Copyright © 2018 Edward W. Watson and Martin M. Culy. All rights reserved. Except for brief quotations in critical publications or reviews, no part of this book may be reproduced in any manner without prior written permission from the publisher. Write: Permissions, Wipf and Stock Publishers, 199 W. 8th Ave., Suite 3, Eugene, OR 97401.

Pickwick Publications
An Imprint of Wipf and Stock Publishers
199 W. 8th Ave., Suite 3
Eugene, OR 97401

www.wipfandstock.com

PAPERBACK ISBN: 978-1-5326-5026-0
HARDCOVER ISBN: 978-1-5326-5027-7
EBOOK ISBN: 978-1-5326-5028-4

Cataloguing-in-Publication data:

Names: Watson, Edward W., author | Culy, Martin M., author

Title: Quoting Corinthians : identifying slogans and quotations in 1 Corinthians / by Edward W. Watson and Martin M. Culy.

Description: Eugene, OR : Pickwick Publications, 2018 | Includes bibliographical references.

Identifiers: ISBN 978-1-5326-5026-0 (paperback) | ISBN 978-1-5326-5027-7 (hardcover) | ISBN 978-1-5326-5028-4 (ebook)

Subjects: LCSH: Bible. Corinthians, 1st—Criticism, interpretation, etc. | Bible. Corinthians, 1st—Quotations.

Classification: LCC BS2675.2 Q7 2018 (print) | LCC BS2675.2 (ebook)

Manufactured in the U.S.A.   NOVEMBER 29, 2018

Scripture quotations marked (NRSV) are from the New Revised Standard Version Bible, copyright © 1989 National Council of the Churches of Christ in the United States of America. Used by permission. All rights reserved worldwide.

Scripture quotations marked (NASB) are taken from the New American Standard Bible®, copyright © 1960, 1962, 1963, 1968, 1971, 1972, 1973, 1975, 1977, 1995 by The Lockman Foundation Used by permission. www.Lockman.org.

Scripture quotations marked (NKJV) are taken from the New King James Version®, copyright © 1982 by Thomas Nelson, Inc. Used by permission. All rights reserved.

Scripture quotations marked (NIV) are taken from the Holy Bible, New International Version®, NIV®. Copyright © 1973, 1978, 1984, 2011 by Biblica, Inc.™ Used by permission of Zondervan. All rights reserved worldwide. www.zondervan.com The "NIV" and "New International Version" are trademarks registered in the United States Patent and Trademark Office by Biblica, Inc.™

Scripture quotations marked (NET) are taken from the NET Bible® copyright ©1996-2017 by Biblical Studies Press, L.L.C. Used by permission. http://netbible.com. All rights reserved.

Scripture quotations marked (ESV) are taken from The Holy Bible, English Standard Version®, copyright © 2001 by Crossway, a publishing ministry of Good News Publishers. Used by permission. All rights reserved.

Scripture quotations marked (NJB) are taken from The New Jerusalem Bible, copyright © 1985 by Darton, Longman & Todd Ltd. and *Les Editions du Cerf.* Used by permission.

Scripture taken from the Modern English Version. Copyright © 2014 by Military Bible Association. Used by permission. All rights reserved.

Scripture quotations marked (HCSB) are taken from the Holman Christian Standard Bible, copyright © 1999, 2000, 2002, 2003 by Holman Bible Publishers, Nashville Tennessee. Used by permission. All rights reserved.

Contents

Preface ix

Chapter 1: The Challenge Before Us 1

Chapter 2: The Rhetoric of Relationship 11

Chapter 3: Refutation and Diatribe 21

Chapter 4: Quotations in Greek Grammar and in Paul's Letters 32

Chapter 5: Reconstructing Corinthian Slogans and Quotations 38

Chapter 6: The Corinthians and Sexuality: Libertinism 47

Chapter 7: The Corinthians and Sexuality: Asceticism 70

Chapter 8: The Corinthians and Community: Appeals to Advantage 84

Chapter 9: The Corinthians and Order: Speaking in Tongues 110

Chapter 10: The Corinthians and Order: Women Speaking in Church 124

Epilogue: Reading Scripture Responsibly 139

Bibliography 143

Author Index 149

Preface

Fully grasping the meaning of any letter can sometimes be challenging. Some writers intentionally leave you to read between the lines, implying things without coming out and saying them directly. A college student writing home to his parents might say, "I nearly froze to death walking to class today!" when what he means to communicate is, "Could you please send me some money to buy a better coat." Even disregarding the tendency that some people have to communicate more indirectly, we have to recognize that in personal letters, *as a rule*, writers do not spell out all of the background information that is necessary to understand what they are saying. They do not have to, because there is a lot of "inside information" that writers assume when writing a letter to someone they know. And it was no different with New Testament letters. This leaves us with a much greater challenge. Since the New Testament letters were not originally written to us, we are far less equipped to read between the lines, because we don't know what information the writer assumed the readers would know! This has all sorts of implications for the study of the New Testament, and one of those implications relates the New Testament writers' use of quotations.

Contrary to popular thinking among beginning Greek students, God did not choose Koine Greek as the language of the New Testament because it was more precise than any other language. Indeed, one of the ways that it is terribly *imprecise* relates to when a Greek writer is quoting someone else. Why? Because the Greek language did not use quotation marks. Let us say that again, when the biblical writers wrote in Greek they did not have the option of using quotation marks! And although there were ways of explicitly marking something as a quotation, writers often relied on their readers to recognize when a common saying or other type of quotation was involved simply by the prior knowledge they brought to the letter. Thus, when modern readers—almost 2000 years removed from the writing of the New

Preface

Testament and from a very different cultural and literary context—read a New Testament book, we potentially run the risk of missing the fact that a biblical writer is quoting someone else's position rather than stating his own. This can have serious implications for how we understand the Bible.

Most scholars stress that Paul's first canonical letter to the church at Corinth contains a number of references to Corinthian positions that are expressed as slogans. Paul was well aware of how the various factions in the church thought from his extensive earlier interaction with them, including a recent letter they had sent to him. And some of the Corinthian positions reflected beliefs that were cause for much concern on Paul's part. In what follows, we will suggest that Paul quotes a number of these positions in 1 Corinthians in order to refute or correct them. This was a common tactic used in ancient Hellenistic rhetoric, particularly when a philosopher or teacher encountered or anticipated misunderstandings among his hearers or students. Since Greek writers often did not explicitly indicate when they were quoting others, however, we are left with the question of how to determine when Paul was doing so in 1 Corinthians.

This study is an outgrowth of research that I (Edward) have done over the years in preparation for teaching the Pauline Epistles and other courses on the New Testament that rely on English Bible translations, working on a couple of related research projects,[1] and serving as editor-in-chief of the New Testament for the Modern English Version translation project (MEV). I am grateful to a number of students who have assisted me with research for this study, all of whom were part of my "Paul: Mission and Message" courses in 2015 and 2016: Josue Cevallos, Lisa Daniels, Christopher Dart, Starlencia Hoye, Joy-Anne Thompson, Vivian Castillo, Kimberly DeVore, and Shan Elahi. These students, along with my research assistant Geoffrey Graff who also provided valuable help, represent the type of student for which this study is designed: intermediate students of biblical interpretation, translation practice and theory, historical critical analysis, ancient rhetoric, or theology.

I (Martin) was intrigued when Ed asked me to join him on this project. The issues we address in what follows reflect challenges that I wrestled with serving with Wycliffe Bible Translators beginning in the 1980s. I later had the privilege of reviewing Rollin Ramsaran's work on maxims in 1

---

1. Watson, "A History of Influence," 15–30; idem, *Paul, His Roman Audience, and the Adopted People of God.*

Preface

Corinthians,[2] which I believe sheds considerable light on what is going on in Paul's letter. It is my hope that what follows will help not only scholars and students of the New Testament, but also Bible translators around the world as they face the challenging task of putting Paul's complex arguments in 1 Corinthians into other languages.

Beyond this, we both hope that as readers work through the process this book presents, they will be able to take a significant step forward toward the goal of "rightly explaining the word of truth" (2 Tim 2:15, NRSV), not only in terms of what 1 Corinthians meant for the original audience and what it means for us today, but also in terms of being better prepared to identify potential quotes in other New Testament letters.

---

2. Culy, review of Hays, Murphy-O'Connor, Hunt, and Ramsaran, 394–98.

1

The Challenge Before Us

> *The interpretation of 1 Corinthians is greatly conditioned by the exegete's assessment of the situation at Corinth, because Paul's words can mean different things when read against various backgrounds. Hence the need to determine as objectively as possible the positions adopted by the Corinthians.* — Jerome Murphy-O'Connor

Why should we study the places in 1 Corinthians where Paul might be quoting Corinthians?[1] The answer may surprise you! Identifying when Paul is quoting Corinthians may actually significantly affect our understanding of 1 Corinthians. And, consequently, it may also affect how we live and worship as followers of Jesus Christ. What we will discuss below is important not simply for scholars, but for people in the pews. Perhaps when you encounter a book like this, particularly if you are forced to read it for a course you are taking, your first questions are, "So what? How does this have any relevance to my life?" Given the importance of such questions, we will address them initially in the paragraphs that follow and also engage them throughout this book, rather than expecting readers to figure out the relevance of this study on their own.

---

1. We use the phrase "quoting Corinthians" rather than "quoting the Corinthians" to recognize that Paul is not responding to quotations originating from the Corinthian church as a whole, but rather to quotations that are coming from some Corinthians whose thinking is off track.

First Things First

Scholarly treatments of 1 Corinthians often refer to Corinthian "slogans." Virtually all scholars agree that Paul at times in 1 Corinthians cites the positions of particular factions within the church with whom he disagrees before qualifying or correcting their faulty thinking. The label "slogan" is actually a broad category (similar to the term "maxim," which was used in the ancient Greek rhetorical handbooks), which includes established expressions of dogma, mottos, common sayings, and perhaps even brief ways of capturing the gist of an opponent's way of thinking.[2] Thus, although the slogans typically represent actual stated positions of various groups in the church in Corinth, at times when Paul "quotes" the Corinthians, he may be putting their thinking or behavior into a succinct statement that he has *himself* created as a convenient way of engaging their position. In other words, Paul may at times quote the Corinthians *as if* they had said something that they had never explicitly stated, but his quote nevertheless accurately represents their position. In either case, the intended Corinthian readers would have easily recognized their own slogan or Paul's pithy summary of behavior or thinking within the church.[3]

It is indisputable that Paul refers to his readers' positions in 1 Corinthians. For example, to deal with quarrels within the church that he learned about from oral reports (1:11), Paul appears to quote the slogans of some of his readers in 1:12: "What I mean is that each of you says, 'I belong to Paul,' or 'I belong to Apollos,' or 'I belong to Cephas,' or 'I belong to Christ.'" He then seeks to correct the flawed thinking of his readers in 1:13: "Has Christ been divided? Was Paul crucified for you? Or were your baptized in the name of Paul?"[4] Although these quotations are easy to spot, other potential slogans or quotations are far less obvious.[5] This is where our challenge lies.

---

2. Klein, Blomberg, and Hubbard describe slogans as Paul's quotations of "views held by some in Corinth that he wishes to dispute" (*Introduction to Biblical Interpretation*, 436).

3. Jay Smith's helpful definition of a slogan also allows for this possibility: "a motto of a particular group or point of view at Corinth, or at least a motto that Paul was using to represent their position or attitudes" (Smith, "Slogans in 1 Corinthians," 82).

4. Even in 1:12 there is debate over whether the slogans represent quotations of actual Corinthian statements or represent Paul's creative way of referring to the factional thinking and behavior in the church. We will return to an analysis of 1:12 in chapter 5 below.

5. Another clear quotation, although it is not clear if it is a direct or indirect quote, can be seen in 15:12: "Now if Christ is proclaimed as raised from the dead, how can some of you say there is no resurrection of the dead?"

The Challenge Before Us

We should rightly assume that the Corinthian readers would have easily recognized when Paul was referring to their own positions (quoting them). They would have then been well prepared to hear how Paul reacted to those positions.[6] Since we are not first-century Corinthians, however, we are left to attempt to put ourselves in their shoes and use every tool at our disposal to determine when Paul was quoting them.

What Is at Stake?

Why is our study so important? Plain and simple, identifying embedded slogans in 1 Corinthians will significantly impact our interpretation of the relevant passages. It is, therefore, imperative that we determine *where* Paul is using slogans or quotations so that we will be able to separate what Paul is saying from what the Corinthians have said. As Smith rightly points out,

> The slogans embedded in 1 Corinthians must be ferreted out, and Paul's reaction to them must be ascertained. Otherwise one risks endorsing what Paul rejected (or perhaps rejecting what Paul endorsed). Such a mistake could have disastrous consequences for Christian theology, ethics, and witness.[7]

For most Christians, the only way of determining whether a biblical writer is quoting someone else or not is to consult the Bible translation they normally use. English readers tend to assume that if there are quotation marks, there is a quote; if there are no quotation marks, no quote. Bible translation, however, *always* involves interpretation; and this is particularly true when the original writers sometimes quoted other sources without explicitly identifying that material as a quotation. How do we know when the biblical writers were quoting someone else? Unlike the "clear" quotations we find in 1 Cor 1:12, most of the other potential quotes in 1 Corinthians are not conveniently introduced by a helpful expression like, "You say." And English translations of the relevant passages do not always agree on when Paul is quoting Corinthians and when he is expressing his own opinion.

For example, in 1 Cor 7:1, Paul refers to questions that were raised in a letter from Corinth. Some translations put the issue addressed in 7:1 in

---

6. Smith notes that in citing a Corinthian "slogan" Paul may not be quoting the expression verbatim; "Slogans in 1 Corinthians," 83; contra Murphy-O'Connor who believes that all the slogans represent precise sayings of Paul's Corinthian opponents; *Keys to First Corinthians*, 25.

7. Smith, "Slogans in 1 Corinthians," 71.

quotation marks, indicating that Paul is quoting Corinthians: "Now concerning the matters about which you wrote: 'It is well for a man not to touch a woman'" (NRSV). Paul then objects to this slogan in 7:2–5. The NIV (1984) and NASB, on the other hand, translate the clause without quotations marks, leaving the impression that the opinion is actually *Paul's* perspective, or perhaps leaving it to the reader to decide: "Now concerning the things about which you wrote, it is good for a man not to touch a woman" (NASB). This, of course, creates other problems for Bible readers as they try to interpret Paul's subsequent words. We will return to this passage in more detail in chapter 7.

Even when translators agree that Paul is quoting Corinthians, however, they do not always agree on where the quote begins and ends. Both the NRSV and the NIV 1984, for example, make it clear through the use of quotation marks that Paul is quoting a Corinthian slogan in 1 Cor 6:13, but the NIV 2011 and NET extend the quotation further than the NRSV or NIV 1984:

> "Food is meant for the stomach and the stomach for food," and God will destroy both one and the other. The body is meant not for fornication but for the Lord, and the Lord for the body. (NRSV)

> "Food for the stomach and the stomach for food"—but God will destroy them both. The body is not meant for sexual immorality, but for the Lord, and the Lord for the body. (NIV 1984)

> "You say, 'Food for the stomach and the stomach for food, and God will destroy them both.' The body, however, is not meant for sexual immorality but for the Lord, and the Lord for the body." (NIV 2011)

> "Food is for the stomach and the stomach is for food, but God will do away with both." The body is not for sexual immorality, but for the Lord, and the Lord for the body. (NET)

Other versions, like the NASB, do not use quotation marks at all in this passage, leaving the impression that the first clause is also part of *Paul's* opinion, rather than something that some of the Corinthians were teaching:

> "Food is for the stomach and the stomach is for food, but God will do away with both of them. Yet the body is not for immorality, but for the Lord, and the Lord is for the body (NASB)."

Readers of the NIV 2011 or NET will assume that the first part of Paul's response to the Corinthians' slogan is not "God will destroy both one and the other" (NRSV), but rather, "The body is meant not for fornication but for the Lord, and the Lord for the body" (NRSV). And it is the Corinthians who are maintaining that "God will do away with both" (NET) the food and the stomach. Thus, the NRSV and NIV 1984 present a very different way of understanding 1 Cor 6:13 than the NIV 2011 and the NET. Which is right? Or, to quote Paul's words elsewhere, "What then are we to say about these things?" (Rom 8:31).

The answer should be obvious: It is critical that we determine, to the best of our ability, when Paul or other biblical writers are quoting someone else's position. While commentators routinely assume that Corinthian slogans are embedded in the text of 1 Corinthians, most fail to provide any clear criteria for identifying them.[8] In what follows, we will attempt to develop an objective method[9] for determining when Paul is quoting Corinthian positions that students of the Bible can apply to this and other New Testament letters. Fortunately, we will not have to sail these rough interpretative waters alone, since others have gone before us and have offered important guidance. A few influential earlier studies are particularly important.[10]

Major Monographs on Corinthian Quotations

Hurd, John C., Jr. *The Origin of 1 Corinthians*. London: SPCK, 1965.

> This publication represents Hurd's doctoral dissertation from Yale University. Although the work is dated, it is significant because it represents the first serious effort to deal with Paul's use of quotations to represent Corinthian positions. Hurd identifies eight passages with Corinthian quotations.

Mitchell, Margret M. *Paul and the Rhetoric of Reconciliation: An Exegetical Investigation of the Language and Composition of 1 Corinthians*. Louisville: Westminster John Knox, 1992.

---

8. See Omanson, "Acknowledging Paul's Quotations," 201–2.

9. Or, at least, a *more* objective method.

10. We will note some other important works on specific verses in 1 Corinthians later as we examine relevant passages.

Mitchell's work is important because it demonstrates that 1 Corinthians uses deliberative rhetoric to persuade the Corinthian community to become unified by following a specific course of action that will bring reconciliation to a factionalized church. She deals with Paul's arguments throughout the letter and indicates how these function to dissuade factions within the community.

Murphy-O'Connor, Jerome. *Keys to First Corinthians: Revisiting the Major Issues*. Oxford: Oxford University Press, 2009.

This volume is made up of articles written by Murphy-O'Connor that were originally published from 1997–2008, some of which deal with potential slogans in 1 Corinthians. Murphy-O'Connor serves as an important pioneer in this area of research.

Ramsaran, Rollin A. *Liberating Words: Paul's Use of Rhetorical Maxims in 1 Corinthians 1–10*. Valley Forge, PA: Trinity, 1996.

Ramsaran's important study suggests that "maxims were not only an integral part of the social and moral thought world of Paul and the Corinthians, but also played an important role in their ongoing discussions."[11] Although we will not make use of a fine distinction between slogans and maxims in this study, Ramsaran appropriately notes that "the sayings of the Corinthians to which Paul responds were more than just 'slogans' that provided a rallying cry for a specific faction. Instead, as 'maxims' conveying moral counsel, they carried an obvious implicit claim: the Corinthians who used the maxims possessed special wisdom."[12] Paul, thus, responds in an appropriate fashion, using maxim argumentation himself to convey true wisdom from God.

Siebermann, Paul. "The Question of Slogans in 1 Corinthians." PhD diss., Baylor University, 1997.

Siebenmann adds to the work of others before him by expanding the criteria for evaluating slogans, examining seventeen putative slogans in 1 Corinthians.

---

11. Culy, review of Hays, Murphy-O'Connor, Hunt, and Ramsaran, 398.
12. Ibid.

Important Articles on Corinthian Slogans

Burk, Denny. "Discerning Corinthian Slogans through Paul's Use of the Diatribe in 1 Corinthians 6:12–20." *Bulletin for Biblical Research* 18/1 (2008) 99–121.

> Denny Burk analyzes the features of diatribe in 1 Cor 6 to show how Paul uses this rhetorical strategy to address issues in the church at Corinth. He points out that Paul is responding to actual opinions expressed by real people. He also presents an exegesis of the passage in light of the Corinthian slogans he identifies.

Dodd, B. J. "Paul's Paradigmatic 'I' and 1 Corinthians 6.12." *Journal for the Study of the New Testament* 59 (1995) 39–58.

> Dodd argues against the opinion that 6:12 is a slogan and he maintains that everything in the chapter comes from Paul.

Fotopoulos, John. "Arguments Concerning Food Offered to Idols: Corinthian Quotations and Pauline Refutations in a Rhetorical *partitio* (1 Corinthians 8:1–9)." *Catholic Biblical Quarterly* 67/4 (October 2005) 611–31.

> Fotopoulos notes the apparent contradictions in 1 Cor 8:1–9, but he maintains that these contradictions can be attributed to Paul's use of the rhetorical form, *partitio*, which contains Corinthian quotations interspersed with Paul's refutations. This allows for readers to interpret 1 Cor 8:1—11:1 as a coherent Pauline exposition about food sacrificed to idols. Fotopoulos provides an introduction to the nature and use of the *partitio*, and includes a chart of proposed Corinthian quotations in 1 Corinthians.

Fotopoulos, John. "The Rhetorical Situation, Arrangement, and Argumentation of 1 Corinthians 8:1–13: Insights into Paul's Instructions on Idol-Food in Greco-Roman Context." *The Greek Orthodox Theological Review* 47 (2002) 165–98.

> Fotopoulos argues for the presence of maxims in 1 Cor 8. He examines the rhetorical situation, arrangement, and argumentation of 1 Cor 8:1–13 and demonstrates that Paul uses the *partitio* to refute the sentiments expressed by the Corinthians.

Lambrecht, J. "Paul's Reasoning in 1 Corinthians 6:12-20." *Ephemerides Theologicae Lovanienses* 85/4 (2009) 479–86.

> Lambrecht builds on earlier work to do further analysis of 1 Cor 6:12. He concludes that there are slogans in 6:12–13, but argues against the presence of a slogan in 6:18.

Mackie, S. D. "The Two Tables of the Law and Paul's Ethical Methodology in 1 Corinthians 6:12-20 and 10:23—11:1." *Catholic Biblical Quarterly* 75/2 (2013) 315–34.

> Mackie argues for the presence of maxims (slogans) in 6:12–20 and 10:23—11:1, and discusses several theories concerning their sources. He maintains that the maxims may have originated from Paul himself, or from someone who formulated them based on his teaching. He also notes the possibility that these maxims go back to the sayings of Jesus.

Murphy-O'Connor, J. "Corinthian Slogans in 1 Cor 6:12-20." *Catholic Biblical Quarterly* 40/3 (July 1978) 391–96.

> Murphy-O'Connor argues that there is a slogan embedded in 6:18. This article is widely considered seminal work on the subject.

Omanson, Roger L. "Acknowledging Paul's Quotations." *The Bible Translator* 43/2 (April 1992) 201–13.

> Omanson's goal was to determine if an objective method could be established for determining where quotations are being used in Paul's letters. He concludes that an objective method is beyond our reach,[13] but goes on to offer 19 possible slogans in 1 Corinthians, some of which other scholars have not noticed (e.g., 2:15–16; 4:6; 6:18; and 11:2).

Smith, Jay E. "The Roots of a 'Libertine' Slogan in 1 Corinthians 6:18." *Journal of Theological Studies* (April 2008) 63–95.

> Smith analyzes the social, cultural, and religious elements present within the church at Corinth and shows how they are connected to the proposed slogans in 1 Corinthians. He argues that the slogans were constructed by the convergence of two tributaries: a non-Christian or Hellenistic-Roman stream (including popular philosophy and incipient Gnosticism) and a Christian or Jesuanic current, flowing mainly from Paul.

---

13. Omanson, "Acknowledging Paul's Quotations," 203.

Smith, Jay E. "Slogans in 1 Corinthians." *Bibliotheca Sacra* 167 (January–March 2010) 68–88.

In this important article, Smith goes beyond his earlier work to argue that Paul is using Corinthians slogans not only in 6:12–20, but in many other passages in the letter as well. He presents helpful criteria for identifying slogans in 1 Corinthians and concludes with a chart indicating which verses in 1 Corinthians are considered slogans and which scholars concur with his analysis.

Dialogue Partners

The following fifteen modern commentaries will be used in chapters 5–10, where we will examine whether the commentator identified a slogan or quotation in the text and investigate how each interpreted the passage:[14]

Barrett, C. K. *The First Epistle to the Corinthians*. Black's New Testament Commentary. Peabody, MA: Hendrickson, 1968.

Blomberg, Craig. *1 Corinthians*. NIV Application Commentary. Grand Rapids: Zondervan, 1995.

Brookins, Timothy A., and Bruce W. Longenecker. *1 Corinthians 1–9: A Handbook on the Greek Text; 1 Corinthians 10–16: A Handbook on the Greek Text*. Baylor Handbook on the Greek New Testament. Waco: Baylor University Press, 2016.

Bruce, F. F. *1 and 2 Corinthians*. New Century Bible Commentary. Grand Rapids: Eerdmans, 1971.

Ciampa, Roy E., and Brian S. Rosner. *The First Letter to the Corinthians*. Pillar New Testament Commentary. Grand Rapids: Eerdmans, 2010.

Conzelmann, Hans. *1 Corinthians: A Commentary on the First Epistle to the Corinthians*. Translated by J. W. Leitch. Hermeneia. Philadelphia: Fortress, 1975.

Fee, Gordon D. *The First Epistle to the Corinthians*. New International Commentary on the New Testament. Grand Rapids: Eerdmans, 1987.

---

14. These works will be cited by author and page number only in what follows. Given the complexity of the issues involved, it was not always possible to identify precisely where an individual commentator stood on a particular issue. We have attempted to provide an overall analysis of the number of scholars supporting each view, while recognizing that we have at times had to generalize to do so or have merely noted how scholars appear to lean on a particular issue.

Fitzmyer, Joseph A. *First Corinthians: A New Translation with Introduction and Commentary.* Anchor Yale Bible Commentary. New Haven, CT: Yale University Press, 2008.

Garland, David E. *1 Corinthians.* Baker Exegetical Commentary on the New Testament. Grand Rapids: Baker Academic, 2003.

Hays, Richard B. *First Corinthians.* Interpretation. Louisville: John Knox, 1997.

Keener, Craig S. *1–2 Corinthians.* The New Cambridge Bible Commentary. New York: Cambridge University Press, 2005.

Talbert, Charles. *Reading Corinthians: A Literary and Theological Commentary on 1 and 2 Corinthians.* New York: Crossroad, 1989.

Taylor, Mark. *1 Corinthians: An Exegetical and Theological Exposition of Scripture.* The New American Commentary. Nashville: B&H, 2014.

Thiselton, Anthony C. *The First Epistle to the Corinthians: A Commentary on the Greek Text.* New International Greek Testament Commentary. Grand Rapids: Eerdmans, 2000.

Witherington, Ben, III. *Conflict and Community in Corinth: A Socio-Rhetorical Commentary on 1 and 2 Corinthians.* Grand Rapids: Eerdmans, 1995.

Charting a Course

Before setting out on our interpretive journey, we need to chart a course to help ensure that we reach our destination. We will begin by examining Paul's relationship with the church at Corinth more fully, and consider how he gained knowledge of the issues in Corinth that he is responding to in 1 Corinthians. We will then examine Paul's methods for refuting the faulty thinking of the various factions in Corinth. Since some scholars see characteristics of diatribe in Paul's language, and the use of quotations fits very well with the fundamental nature of diatribe, we will need to look more closely at this ancient form of rhetoric. Finally, to complete the groundwork for examining potential slogans and quotations in 1 Corinthians, we will need to consider how ancient Greek writers introduced material from other sources so that we can establish criteria for determining when Paul may be quoting Corinthians in his letter. At that point, we will be prepared to consider the primary passages in 1 Corinthians where quotations may occur, along with Paul's response to them. Finally, we will highlight the theological and practical implications of recognizing Corinthian quotations within Paul's argument.

2

The Rhetoric of Relationship

Corinth: A City of Opportunity

First-century Corinth was the jewel of southern Greece. Built upon an isthmus, Corinth benefited from two harbors, making it the main trade route between Rome and the East. When sailors arrived in the city from either harbor, they were met with every kind of opportunity and temptation in a city well-known for its prosperity, trade, materialism, temples, and prostitutes. This was the city that the apostle Paul came to from Athens in the middle of the first century (Acts 18:1). There, he met Aquila and his wife Priscilla, who had recently relocated to Corinth from Rome.

Figures 1 and 2: Left is the ancient *Diolkos*, the rutted road between the two ports of Corinth. While sailors enjoyed the perks of Corinth, ships would be unloaded in one port and then slaves would drag the ships two miles across the isthmus so that sailors could avoid the treacherous sail around the isthmus. Right is the modern Corinth Canal.

Since Paul shared the same tent making profession as Aquila and Priscilla, they worked together in Corinth while Paul preached in the synagogue every Sabbath (Acts 18:2–4). Although Paul's success in Corinth was limited among the Jews, he had many opportunities with the Corinthian Gentiles who were more open to new ideas and religions. Paul stayed in Corinth, establishing the church and teaching the word of God for a year and a half (Acts 18:5–18).

Figures 3 and 4: The remains of the Corinthian *agora* where Paul, Aquila, and Priscilla would have likely set up their trade of tent making.

The significant length of time that Paul ministered in Corinth is important. It was during this time that he developed close relationships with the young believers there as the founder and shepherd of a new congregation. We know from Acts 18 and 1 Cor 1 that Crispus, who served as an official of the synagogue, became a believer together with his household and Paul baptized them. Additionally, Sosthenes, another synagogue official, was likely beaten for his relationship with Paul and the church. This same Sosthenes appears to have later co-written 1 Corinthians with Paul. Gaius is another individual from the Corinthian church whom Paul baptized (1 Cor 1:14) and who later hosted Paul when he came from Macedonia on his way to Jerusalem after his third missionary journey (likely 56–57 CE), during which time Paul wrote his letter to the church in Rome (Rom 16:23). One other person of note in Corinth is Erastus, the city treasurer, who sent his greetings to the church in Rome when Paul sent them a letter (Rom 16:23). He is noteworthy not only because his position in the city shows the degree to which the gospel had penetrated the city, but also because of the modern day inscription that has been discovered in ancient Corinth that bears his name. These examples help illustrate how productive Paul's time in Corinth was. More than that, they remind us that Paul had many personal relationships with individuals in the church in Corinth. His letter to them, which we know as 1 Corinthians, then, is not a letter to strangers. It is a letter to people whom he knows and loves, and whose situation he is very well acquainted with.

Figure 5: This Latin inscription, dating to the first century CE, reads: "Erastus for the office of aedile laid this pavement at his own expense." This is almost certainly the same Erastus mentioned in Rom 16:23 since it is very unlikely that there could be two men by the name of Erastus who served in Corinth as an aedile (city treasurer) around the time of Paul.

When Paul moved on from Corinth (Acts 18:18), he left a community that was vibrant and growing, but, as we will see from his later correspondence with them, they were also a community that was very open to a wide range of ideas whether from inside or outside of the church. As a result of such openness, the Corinthian church developed various divisions that were expressed in leadership factions, class structure issues, and conflicting worship styles. These divisions created problems for the church that Paul needed to address in his letters.

Paul's correspondence with the Corinthians may be viewed as the most intimate and colorful of all of his letters, reflecting his well-established relationship with the Corinthians and his intense pastoral concern for the destructive thinking among them. His letters reveal an apostle who at times is so frustrated with this church that his words seem to be screaming from the page. Paul's mood in 1 Corinthians, in particular, reflects his absolute refusal to give up the gains he has made for the gospel in Corinth.

The issues reflected in Paul's letters to Corinth are both diverse and specific, the latter of which can make application for the modern reader somewhat tricky. Thus, before we move on it will be helpful to introduce some general background of 1 Corinthians and examine further the personal relationship reflected in the communication between Paul and the Corinthians after he left the city and moved on in his missionary ministry.

Paul and the Corinthians

Moving through the chronology found in the book of Acts, it appears that Paul founded the church in Corinth in the year of 50–51 or 51–52 CE. Several important notes from Acts 18 support this dating. First, upon arriving in Corinth Paul met Aquila and Priscilla, who had recently come to the city after the emperor Claudius issued an edict forcing Jews to leave Rome (Acts 18:1–2). According to the Roman historian Suetonius, this expulsion likely took place around the year 49 CE.[1] Additionally, we read in Acts 18:12–17 that Paul, while in Corinth, was brought before the judgment seat of the proconsul Gallio. We know from an inscription found at Delphi dating to the mid-first century that Gallio was named proconsul by the Emperor Claudius in late 51 CE and served in this position for just over one year.[2] Finally, we are told that Paul stayed in Corinth for a year and a half (Acts 18:11). Thus, the period during which Paul lived and ministered in Corinth can be fairly securely established to 50–52 CE.

---

1. Support for this view is found in the *Lives of the Twelve Caesars*, where "Christ" has likely been misspelled: "Since the Jews constantly made disturbances at the instigation of Chrestus, he [Claudius] expelled them from Rome" (Seutonius, *Claudius* 25).

2. This date is one of the most certain in the New Testament and plays an important role in the reconstruction of the chronology of Paul's life and ministry.

Figures 6 and 7: The remains of the *bema* seat where Paul would have been brought before Gallio. The stone on the bottom left represents the place where the accused would stand before the tribunal.

After Paul left Corinth and moved on to other ministry opportunities, his relationship with the church at Corinth continued to develop. It appears that not long after he departed, he heard something that raised concerns about the church and felt the need to write a letter to deal with sexual immorality in the church. Paul refers to this letter in 1 Cor 5:9 where he states, "I wrote to you in my letter not to associate with sexually immoral persons." This first letter from Paul to Corinth is no longer extant, and is therefore sometimes referred to as the "lost letter."

As time went on, Paul continued to "pastor from a distance" by corresponding with the church at Corinth. At some point, a group of people from Corinth, whom he refers to as "Chloe's people," brought a report to him while he was ministering in Ephesus (1:11–12). Around the same time, the Corinthians wrote a letter to him in which they asked several questions about a variety of issues (7:1). As a result of the oral reports from Chloe's people and the Corinthians' letter, Paul wrote his *second* letter to the Corinthians (as far as we know), which we ironically know as "1 Corinthians." This letter was likely written from Ephesus around 54 CE.

Our glimpse into Paul's relationship with the church at Corinth, however, does not end with what we see in 1 Corinthians and Acts. In 2 Corinthians, we discover that due to strong opposition that had emerged in Corinth, Paul was moved to make what appears to be an emergency visit to Corinth from Ephesus, across the Aegean Sea (ca. 55 CE). Unfortunately, this visit did not go well, to put it mildly.[3] Paul was significantly wronged

---

3. Furnish calls it "a disaster" (Furnish, *II Corinthians*, 159).

by some individual, likely through slander (2 Cor 2:5–11),[4] and he refers to this time as a "painful" visit (2 Cor 2:1–2). Following this painful visit, with his apostolic authority in question, Paul wrote a third letter to defend his apostleship. This letter was apparently very polemical, as he sought to rebuke the Corinthians for their openness toward those who would oppose him. Paul refers to this letter as the "tearful" letter (2 Cor 2:3–4), which he likely wrote around 55 CE. Many scholars believe that this letter has been lost, but others have suggested that the "tearful" letter has been preserved in 2 Cor 10–13, which would account for the significant shift in tone between 2 Cor 1–9 and 2 Cor 10–13. If this is the case, then our current edition of 2 Corinthians is made up of a combination of two different letters.[5]

Paul's "tearful" letter rebuking the Corinthians for their openness to those who opposed him seems to have been effective in bringing repentance from their rebellion (2 Cor 7:8–12). After his cordial relationship with the church had been restored, Paul felt confident enough to write a final letter, which has been referred to as the "cheerful" letter due to its dissimilar tone from the "tearful letter." This letter, which some scholars maintain is found in 2 Cor 1–9, seems to have been written while Paul was traveling from Macedonia before he arrived in Corinth in 56 CE to pick up the collection that the Corinthians have been gathering for the poor in Jerusalem (see Acts 20:2–3; 2 Cor 8:1–15; 9:1–15). Paul stayed in Corinth for three months on this occasion, residing with Gaius (Rom 16:23) during the winter of 56/57 CE. It was during this time that he wrote his letter to the Romans (Rom 15:22–33).

---

4. See Harris, *Second Epistle to the Corinthians*, 225–27; cf. Barnett, *The Second Epistle to the Corinthians*, 124; Furnish, *II Corinthians*, 164, 166–68.

5. The change in tone at 2 Cor 10 certainly need not indicate that 2 Corinthians is a composite of two earlier documents, and there are plenty of scholars who argue strongly for the literary integrity of 2 Corinthians. Among recent commentators, see, e.g., Witherington, 328–29; Kistemaker, *Exposition*, 14–15; Barnett, *The Second Epistle to the Corinthians*, 15–24; Garland, *2 Corinthians*, 33–44; Hafemann, *2 Corinthians*, 31–33. Ultimately, this debate has no bearing on the present study.

The Rhetoric of Relationship

A History of Interaction with Corinth

50–51 CE	Paul founds the church at Corinth (see Acts 18:1–11)
52–53 CE	Paul writes *Letter #1*: "the lost letter" (1 Cor 5:9)
53–54 CE	The Corinthians write to Paul (1 Cor 7:1); Chloe's people bring a report to Paul (1 Cor 1:11–12)
54 CE	Paul writes *Letter #2* (1 Corinthians) to respond to oral reports and deal with issues raised by the church
55 CE	Paul makes a "painful" visit to Corinth where his apostleship is challenged (2 Cor 2:1)
55 CE	Paul writes *Letter #3* ("tearful" letter) to defend his apostleship (2 Cor 2:4; now lost or perhaps 2 Cor 10–13)
55/56 CE	Paul writes *Letter #4* ("cheerful" letter) from Macedonia before arriving in Corinth to pick up the collection to take to Jerusalem (2 Cor 1–9 or 2 Cor 1–13)

Regardless of how we sort out the question of whether 2 Corinthians originated as a single letter or represents the combination of two of Paul's earlier letters, this overall reconstruction of Paul's interaction with the Corinthians over the course of approximately five years illustrates the intimate nature of their relationship, a relationship that is perhaps unique in the New Testament.[6] Their relationship was firmly established during the extended period of time while Paul was "planting" the church and it continued to develop through what appears to have been a free flow of dialogue—through oral messages and written correspondence—between them over the span of several years. During this time, we know that Paul wrote at least four letters to the Corinthians.

The Rhetoric of Relationship

When we examine 1 Corinthians, it is easy to see that prior oral and written correspondence serves as the main impetus for this letter.[7] Many of

---

6. Note, however, the extensive personal interaction between Paul and the church in Ephesus (see, e.g., Acts 20:31).

7. See Hurd's analysis and reconstruction of both the oral reports from Chloe's people to which Paul responds and material that replies to the queries raised by the Corinthians'

the topics found in chapters 1–6 are clearly based on reports from Chloe's people (1:11).[8] The other half of the letter (chapters 7–15) primarily appears to include Paul's responses to specific issues raised by the Corinthians themselves in a letter they had sent to him.[9] The letter as a whole, then, points to extensive interaction between the two parties and makes it clear that it is a highly "occasional" letter.[10]

Delegations from Corinth kept Paul up to date on specific situations[11] and raised concerns orally relating to disunity, sexual ethics, and the Lord's Supper that were plaguing the church.[12] We see evidence for this at several points:

---

letter (*The Origin of 1 Corinthians*, 61–211).

8. It should be noted, however, that the letter is not so structured that some issues based on the oral reports do not freely bleed over into the second half of the letter. Mitchell has effectively demonstrated that 1 Corinthians is a deliberative letter in which Paul addresses many issues dividing the Corinthian congregation by seeking to persuade the church to unify in the common interest of the body (*Paul and the Rhetoric of Reconciliation*, 20–68).

9. Thiselton (483) notes the striking difference in tone between 5:1–6:20 and 7:1–11:1, which he attributes to the first section of Paul's letter dealing with issues with which the Corinthians did not invite Paul's counsel and opinion and those issues in which they appeal to Paul's wisdom and pastoral advice.

10. When we refer to the letter as "occasional," we mean that the letter was written to specific people at a specific time about specific issues. In other words, there was a particular "occasion" that led Paul to write the letter. Modern readers must take this into account when reading and applying a biblical letter to their own context.

11. It should be noted that Paul's mention in 16:17 about the arrival of Stephanas, Fortunatus, and Achaicus could reveal the names of Chloe's people who provided the oral reports mentioned in 1:11. Yet, by naming Chloe's informants, Paul could be exposing the men to retaliation by the culprits in the church; see Fee, 54. On the other hand, these individuals could simply constitute another means of oral communication and dialogue between Paul and the church. In addition to Chloe's people and the three individuals who traveled from Corinth to visit him, Paul mentions that Aquila and Prisca were with him in Ephesus as he wrote the letter (16:19). These two friends of Paul had been with him in Corinth (Acts 18:2–3) and could add an additional avenue of communication between the church and the apostle. Moreover, Sosthenes is mentioned as a co-author of his letter (1:1–2). If this is the same Sosthenes who served as the leader of the synagogue in Corinth while Paul lived in the city (Acts 18:17), as is likely, then he represents yet another likely source of information regarding what was taking place in the Corinthian church. Finally, the possible visit by Timothy (16:10) and the visit by "the other brothers" mentioned by Paul in his note about Apollos (16:12) provide additional means of correspondence between the apostle and the church.

12. Additionally, Paul's specific knowledge of their circumstances can be seen as he confronts the problems of a man sleeping with his stepmother (1 Cor 5) and of Corinthians taking each other to court (1 Cor 6).

The Rhetoric of Relationship

"*It has been reported to me* that there are quarrels among you" (1:11–12)

"*It is actually reported* that there is sexual immorality among you" (5:1)

"*I hear* that there are divisions among you [about the Lord's Supper]" (11:18)

Paul then responded to these issues in very specific ways; and given the fact that his response (1 Corinthians) was part of an ongoing conversation between the apostle and the church, we can expect that his letter would have been eagerly anticipated by the Corinthians.

Paul also responds, though, to a written letter sent from the church, which raised another set of troubling issues. Paul's responses to those issues begin in 7:1, where he writes: "Now concerning the matters about which you wrote." The phrase, "now concerning" (περὶ δέ, *peri de*), occurs elsewhere in 1 Corinthians and likely serves as a rhetorical marker indicating places where Paul is engaging issues or questions raised in a letter he received from the church in Corinth:

"*Now concerning* the virgins" (7:25)

"*Now concerning* food offered to idols" (8:1)

"*Now concerning* spiritual gifts" (12:1)

"*Now concerning* the collection" (16:1)

"*Now concerning* Apollos" (16:12)[13]

Some maintain that the use of "now concerning" could simply be equivalent to a modern writer using "first," "second," "third," etc., to organize points of discussion. In this view, the phrase would merely introduce the next topic that Paul will address. It is more likely, however, that in each of the five examples listed above, "now concerning" (περὶ δέ, *peri de*) is short for a longer expression, which was introduced in 7:1 and therefore need not be repeated in full: "Now concerning the matters about which you wrote."[14]

---

13. Note that Paul uses a similar rhetorical structure in 1 Thessalonians, where instead of responding to questions sent to him in a letter, he answers concerns from the church sent through Timothy (1 Thess 3:6). The same marker—"Now concerning" (περὶ δέ, *peri de*)—indicates Paul's responses to the concerns of the church regarding the issues of love within the church (4:9), those who have died (4:13), and the timing of the Day of the Lord (5:1).

14. The significance of this expression in 1 Corinthians is, not surprisingly, debated; see Hurd, *Origin of 1 Corinthians*, 61–71. Mitchell rightly notes that περὶ δέ (*peri de*) in Greek literature serves as a standard "topic marker" that introduces a subject for which

The sense in 7:25, then, for example, would be "*Now concerning* virgins *about which you wrote.*"

In addition to the above explicit references to oral reports and responses to issues raised in writing by the Corinthians, Paul indicates knowledge of other information from Corinth that would have required prior communication between someone in the church and Paul. For example, in 11:2 Paul commends the Corinthians "because you remember me in everything and maintain the traditions just as I handed them on to you." And in 15:12 Paul states, "Now if Christ is proclaimed as raised from the dead, how can some of you say there is no resurrection of the dead?" These two examples—not to mention Paul's awareness that some were "baptizing on behalf of the dead" (15:29)—reveal Paul's knowledge of further practices and beliefs found in the Corinthian church that must have been relayed to the apostle through oral reports or through written correspondence.

Based on all the above evidence, we see that Paul had a dynamic relationship with the church at Corinth. His theological critique of the various misguided views that some of the Corinthian Christians had embraced flows out of the intimate engagement and longstanding relationship that he had enjoyed with this specific church. As a shepherd of this congregation, who was now some distance removed from them, Paul was compelled to rebuke the church strongly when the need arose but was also quick to rejoice over them when they followed his guidance. He offered frank, down-to-earth guidance on issues of sexuality, marriage, worship styles, class structure, and behavior within the church. And, as we will see, in addressing such matters he often appealed to the Corinthians' faulty thinking by quoting them.

---

readers would be familiar. It, therefore, *need not* refer back to the letter sent to Paul beyond its use in 7:1 (*Paul and the Rhetoric of Reconciliation*, 190–91); see also Mitchell, "Concerning Περὶ δέ in 1 Corinthians," 229–56. When we recognize, however, that Paul uses this expression repeatedly, and that in its first reference explicitly connects it to prior correspondence from the Corinthians, it becomes more likely that the final five uses of the expression are shortened versions of what he used in 7:1. There is no need for him to introduce information that he has already shared with the Corinthians (he is writing about matters they have raised in their letter to him).

3

Refutation and Diatribe

Throughout 1 Corinthians Paul appears to quote a claim made by his opponents and then counter it with his own perspective. The slogans or positions he refers to could have easily come to him through the oral reports made by the delegates from Chloe, been included in the earlier letter(s) received by Paul from the church, or simply be based on earlier interaction between Paul and the church. They may even represent Paul's characterization of the Corinthians' flawed thinking.[1] Regardless of the method by which Paul received the claims, the slogans he cites clearly represent teachings, maxims, assertions, or positions embraced by various factions within the church to which Paul feels compelled to respond.

This rhetorical strategy of citing slogans or positions in order to then refute them is consistent with common practices of ancient Hellenistic rhetoricians, and was particularly common in diatribe. Before examining possible cases of Paul's use of Corinthian slogans in 1 Corinthians, we therefore need to survey how this rhetorical strategy was used in Hellenistic diatribe. Next, we need to investigate what features of Greek grammar were used to signal the introduction of direct or indirect discourse (direct or indirect quotations), realizing that at times authors may quote other sources without giving any indication that a citation was being made. This will then serve as the foundation for establishing a methodology for determining when Paul was quoting Corinthians in his letter. Once these issues

---

1. Smith ("Slogans in 1 Corinthians," 79) adds: "The point is that this dialogue between Paul and the Corinthians allows—even demands—subtle echoes within 1 Corinthians of previous events and prior interchanges. It would be surprising if one or more of the Corinthians watchwords did not find their way into 1 Corinthians."

are examined, we will then be ready to address the specific occasions where Paul may employ his opponents' slogans and positions in his letter and the interpretive implications for reading 1 Corinthians.

The Rhetorical Art of Refuting Opponents

Following the influential work of Margaret M. Mitchell, we acknowledge that the purpose of Paul's letter to Corinth was to address a range of issues that were dividing the community, and Paul uses deliberative rhetoric in an effort to persuade the factious church to become united in love.[2] Deliberative rhetoric can be defined as a style of argument that urges an audience to pursue a particular course by pointing out specific actions that the audience should undertake or abstain from in the future.[3] Although there is little doubt that 1 Corinthians represents deliberative rhetoric, we must still identify what specific rhetorical strategies Paul employs and how these strategies may work in conjunction with his quotations of Corinthian slogans or positions.[4]

While it is unknown exactly how much rhetorical training Paul received, his letters suggest that he had at least an intermediate understanding of traditional rhetorical devices. The common rhetorical approach used to refute opponents is found in a fourth-century classical Greek text on rhetoric written by Aphthonius the Sophist, entitled *Preliminary Exercises*, where the teacher instructs his readers on educated discourse.[5] Aphthonius writes, "Refutation (*anaskeuê*) is an overturning of some matter at hand. One should refute what is neither very clear nor what is altogether impossible, but what holds a middle ground. Those engaged in refutation *should first state the false claim* of those who advance it, then add an exposition of

---

2. Mitchell, *Paul and the Rhetoric of Reconciliation*, 20–68.

3. Ibid., 24–25. Ramsaran (*Liberating Words*, 27) rightly notes that "1 Corinthians is deliberative oratory within an epistolary framework."

4. As we move forward in our investigation, we will examine other aspects of rhetoric that may help us to further understand Paul's style of argumentation. For example, in chapter 8, we will examine the work of Fotopoulos, who has noted that Paul's arguments in various places in 1 Corinthians may reflect a rhetorical *partitio*. This is evidenced when Paul enumerates the opponents' positions, both agreed upon and disputed, followed by his own positions. Fotopoulos, "Arguments Concerning Food," 611–31.

5. Although this text dates to the fourth century CE, it represents the classical approach.

the subject."⁶ This closely follows the work traditionally attributed to Hermogenes (2nd cent.),⁷ and is a method of refutation that Paul frequently adopts in his letter to the Corinthians. Paul also appears to adopt a style of refutation reflected in Nicolaus the Sophist, who wrote around the same time as Aphtonius: "Some argue by setting out part by part and others fight against the (opponent's) speech as a whole. To me, part by part seems rather better; for in that way the discourse becomes more contentious."⁸ Like Nicolaus, Paul shows a clear preference for the "part by part" approach to refutation.

Finally, it is important to keep in mind that when ancient authors quoted their opponents they did not always feel compelled to ensure word-for-word precision.⁹ So, again, although we should assume that Paul accurately represents the positions of the Corinthians, his quotations need not be exactly what they had said.¹⁰

In the rhetoric of Paul's day, as in modern rhetoric, an author often alluded to or quoted a saying from another source to confirm his position or support his own point of view. In classical rhetoric, this was known as "confirmation," while the opposite was known as "refutation."¹¹ In Paul's letters we often find him using quotes or allusions to confirm his position, particularly from the Old Testament. A good example is found in 14:21, where Paul appears to utilize a direct quote from the Old Testament prophets as a source of confirmation: "In the law it is written, 'By people of strange tongues and by the lips of foreigners I will speak to this people; yet even then they will not listen to me,' says the Lord." Many English translations offset the passage to alert the reader that this is a direct quotation of an Old Testament verse. At other times, Paul will make use of an Old Testament quote to refute his opponents. A good example is found in 9:9.

---

6. Kennedy, *Progynmasmata*, 101, italics added.

7. Ibid., 79. There are also interesting parallels between how Paul presents his case to the Corinthians and what Aelius Theon (first century) discusses under the heading, "On Thesis." See ibid., 55–57.

8. Ibid., 146.

9. Robertson, *A Grammar of the Greek New Testament*, 1027.

10. It is, in fact, possible that Paul is at times presenting misunderstandings that are *anticipated* based on his limited knowledge rather than current positions that the Corinthians had already espoused. Due to Paul's close association with Corinth, however, and the variety of problems found within the church, it is likely that Paul is dealing with concrete issues and real opinions.

11. See, e.g., Nicolaus the Sophist in Kennedy, *Progynmasmata*, 144–47.

Paul has apparently been criticized for accepting food and drink from those he ministers to (and perhaps other forms of compensation). To refute his opponents' faulty view that such a practice is inappropriate, he quotes the Old Testament: "For it is written in the law of Moses, 'You shall not muzzle an ox while it is treading out the grain.'" Paul also, however, makes use of more distinctive features of rhetoric from his particular milieu, particularly as a key strategy for refutation.

The Ancient Use of the Diatribe

In the past half century, there has been a surge in the study of ancient Hellenistic diatribe and its use by New Testament authors, especially Paul. Few scholars, however, have given much attention to the use of diatribe in 1 Corinthians. This represents a problem that can have significant implications for determining when Paul is quoting Corinthians, since diatribe typically involved a writer or speaker interacting with imaginary opponents, using a question and answer format, addressing hypothetical objections, or refuting faulty thinking. It was thus very well suited for first-century writers who needed to engage problematic thinking in their students . . . or churches! What is important for us is to recognize that if we can establish that Paul is using diatribe at a particular point in his argument, it will help us to recognize when he is dialoguing with Corinthian positions that he desires to correct; and it will tell us that we have come to the type of context where quotations commonly occur.

Without fully recounting the influential argument laid out by Denny Burk on Paul's use of diatribe in 1 Cor 6:12–20, we need to mention a few important points that he makes.[12] Burk convincingly demonstrates that Paul utilizes diatribe in this passage, identifying four out of five features of diatribe.[13] Burk points out that if Paul utilizes diatribe in his argument, it would signal to his readers that he is referring to material that he in some way attributes to the Corinthians. He notes that diatribe makes use of back and forth dialogue between an author and an imaginary interlocutor (a second-person conversation partner embedded in the text). What is distinctive in 1 Cor 6, as Burk points out, is that instead of Paul using the expected second person *singular* to portray the position of the imaginary

---

12. Burk, "Discerning Corinthian Slogans," 99–121.

13. As we will see below, all features need not to be present for an argument to be considered diatribe.

opponent, he uses second person *plural* forms ("you all"), which suggests that the interlocutors in view were not imaginary at all, but rather were actual Corinthians. Paul's twist on conventional diatribe (speaking to a concrete position held by members of his intended audience, rather than utilizing an *imaginary* rhetorical partner) is distinctive. Burk posits that Paul's special adaptation of diatribe is based on the highly occasional nature of the epistle, which flows out of Paul's close familiarity with the audience. He is directly responding to reports from Chloe's household and one or more letters from the Corinthians. It is not surprising, then, that he would make use of a common, powerful form of communication (diatribe) to address the very real issues the church in Corinth was facing. Burk concludes that the intended audience would have picked up on the subtle nuances in Paul's rhetoric, nuances that modern readers and interpreters easily overlook. He goes on to suggest that if his argument is correct, modern translators should include quotations marks, when warranted, to guide modern readers toward appropriate interpretation of 1 Cor 6:12–20.

As we continue in our examination of 1 Corinthians, we will test whether Burk's theories hold true for other putative Corinthian quotations. If features of diatribe are present in 6:12–20, it stands to reason that Paul may use this powerful rhetorical tool elsewhere in 1 Corinthians as he addresses other issues and positions needing correction in the church at Corinth. We will need to examine each text to see if features of diatribe are present that would suggest that Paul is quoting real Corinthian interlocutors. To accomplish this goal we will need to gain a greater understanding of: (1) the characteristics of diatribe;[14] (2) Paul's use of the features associated with diatribe; and (3) Paul's potential variation of standard diatribe in his correction of false thinking in 1 Corinthians.

The Characteristics of Greco-Roman Diatribe

In ancient philosophical schools, the word "diatribe" referred to informal remarks made by a teacher "in which he addressed and rebuked students or refuted logical objections to his teaching."[15] The apostle Paul was certainly familiar with this type of argumentation as seen by his extensive use of

---

14. Since studies of extant primary sources are readily available and lie beyond the scope of our investigation, we will focus on simply summarizing the nature and characteristics of diatribe.

15. Kennedy, *A New History of Classical Rhetoric*, 93.

diatribe in Romans (see below). Although Paul does not seem to use this rhetorical strategy extensively in his other letters, he certainly does not shy away from using *features* of diatribe elsewhere.

The English word "diatribe" is based on the Greek διατριβή (*diatribē*) and is associated with the modern English notions of "conversation," "discourse," "seminar," and "lecture."[16] Unfortunately, modern perspectives on Greco-Roman diatribe have often been vague, and no real consensus has been reached on how and when diatribe came into existence. Many scholars posit that Bion the Borysthenite (3rd cent. BCE) was the founder of the diatribe style of argument,[17] while others point to earlier works that appear to contain characteristics of this rhetorical strategy.[18] Still others argue that diatribe may have had its beginnings in the dialogues of Plato and been built upon the teaching style of Socrates.[19] Whatever its origins, most of the extant sources that exhibit fully developed diatribe (various forms of moral literature and philosophical rhetoric) date from the first century BCE to the early second century CE. Examples of these sources are readily accessible today.[20]

According to Aune, the word diatribe describes "an informal rhetorical mode of argumentation principally characterized by a lively dialogical style including the use of imaginary discussion partners (often abruptly addressed), to whom are attributed hypothetical objections and false conclusions."[21] The goal of this type of instruction was not simply to impart knowledge, but to transform the students or listeners by pointing out the error of their false conclusions and then correcting it.[22] Various methods of argument were employed:

---

16. Aune, *The Westminster Dictionary*, 127.

17. See Schenkeveld, "Diatribe and Dialexis," 233.

18. See Kennedy, *A New History of Classical Rhetoric*, 92. It is likely that there are numerous examples of incipient diatribe, which predate the fully developed diatribe we find later.

19. Schenkeveld, "Diatribe and Dialexis," 296.

20. Although Stowers focuses on Paul's use of diatribe in Romans, he includes an important study of the use of diatribe by ancient writers such as Teles, Musonius, Bion, Epictetus, Seneca, Dio Chrysostom, and Plutarch; see *The Diatribe and Paul's Letter to the Romans*, 226–31. For a fuller discussion of ancient diatribe, see Schenkeveld, "Diatribe and Dialexis," 232ff.

21. Aune, *The Westminster Dictionary*, 127.

22. Stowers, "The Diatribe," 75–76.

Plutarch has used the form of narrating elaborate fictitious diatribes, i.e. scholastic discussions, in order to present his own ideas. The characteristic form of extant diatribes from Teles in the third century BCE onward is that of a lecture or written treatise which discusses common moral-philosophical topics enlivened at various points by fictitious dialogue and questions from imaginary auditors. Diatribes which record actual school activity contain discussions both with real and imaginary discussion partners.[23]

Based upon the study of the extant sources available, diatribe is essentially the rhetoric of refutation in which the author addresses real or anticipated false positions and corrects them. Although no formal structure can be attributed to diatribe,[24] scholars are quick to point out that there are common features that can be clearly identified from extant sources. Aune notes that "the dialogical style of diatribes makes frequent use of imaginary opponents, hypothetical objections, and false conclusions. The questions and objections of the imaginary opponent and the teacher's response oscillate between censure and persuasion. Censure exposes contradiction, error, and ignorance."[25] Stowers adds:

> The diatribal authors simulate direct address in their discourses by creating an imaginary discussion partner, and by means of direct address to their audiences. The dialogical element in the diatribe takes several forms and within limits varies considerably from author to author. One method consists of short exchanges of questions and answers. Often this is in the Socratic manner with the teacher leading the fictitious interlocutor by means of pointed questions, frequently posing absurdities which the interlocutor must strongly reject. This method is prominent in Teles, Epictetus and Dio Chrysostom. Sometimes the interlocutor asks the questions and the teacher answers. A technique of many authors is to string a series of objections and false conclusions from the interlocutor throughout the lecture or treatise. The interlocutor's question draws a false inference from which the author wishes to guard himself or poses a typical objection to the author's line of reasoning. The teacher's answer, then, serves as a transition to a new topic or step in the augmentation. A series of such objections may become a structuring principle for a discourse. Objections

---

23. Ibid., 75.
24. Ibid.
25. Aune, *The New Testament in Its Literary Environment*, 200.

and false conclusions are often rejected with strong negatives or an oath-formula, e.g., *mē genoito* (By no means!).[26]

Although some common elements and characteristics can be gleaned from the sources containing diatribe, it is important to understand that diatribe is a set of rhetorical techniques used for persuasion rather than a formal genre.[27] Consequently, while one should expect to find some features of diatribe when this rhetorical strategy is being employed, not all features need to be present for a text to be considered a diatribe.[28]

Paul's Use of the Features of Diatribe

Since the influential dissertation published by Rudolf Bultmann in 1910,[29] most scholars have come to believe that various characteristics of the diatribe style are utilized by some New Testament authors. Studies have shown, for example, that Paul's letter to the Romans contains many of the classical characteristics associated with diatribe, with features of diatribe being found in Romans 2, 3, 4, 5, 6, 7, 9, 11, and 14 (and possibly elsewhere).[30] A particularly clear example of diatribe is found in Rom 2:17–29, where Paul introduces an imaginary Jewish interlocutor whom he chastises for failing to be a light to the Gentiles. He continues his dialogue with this interlocutor in 3:1–9 and 3:27—4:2, posing rhetorical questions that he then answers, effectively defending God's faithfulness despite human weakness. Often, Paul addresses his imaginary interlocutor in the second person singular in Romans (see 2:1–5; 9:19–21; 11:17–24; 14:4, 10).[31] Moreover, he

---

26. Stowers, "The Diatribe," 75.

27. Stowers's important work on the subject of diatribe has helped create a near consensus among scholars that the term was not used to describe a particular literary genre in antiquity; see ibid., 73; Stowers, *The Diatribe and Paul's Letter to the Romans*, 49; and Porter, "Diatribe," 296–97.

28. Stowers, "The Diatribe," 75.

29. Bultmann, *Der Stil der paulinischen Predigt und die kynisch-stoische Diatribe*. Bultmann's study emphasized the characteristics of Greco-Roman diatribe found in Romans. He proposed that these features reflect Paul's preaching style, which was consistent with the preaching style of popular philosophical speakers. Stowers ("The Diatribe," 73), arguing against Bultmann's conclusion, contends that diatribe did not belong to the polemical style of the popular philosophical preachers, but rather to the teacher-student relationship of the philosophical schools.

30. Porter, "Diatribe," 298.

31. Stowers, "The Diatribe," 81; see also Aune, *The Westminster Dictionary*, 129.

frequently introduces a series of objections and false conclusions that he proceeds to refute (see 6:1, 15; 7:7, 13; 9:14, 19; 11:1, 11, 19), sometimes with an emphatic response like μὴ γένοιτο (*mē genoito*), which is typically translated something like, "not at all," "by no means!" or "never!" (see 6:15).

Aune hypothesizes that Paul likely finds the diatribe method helpful in Romans because he was less familiar with the concrete situations in Rome. Therefore, the style would prove more useful than it would in other churches, like Corinth, where Paul had stronger relational ties and fuller information regarding their situation.[32] Although Aune's position makes sense of Paul's more frequent use of hypothetical questions and answers in Romans, as well as frequent introductions of objections and false conclusions, which likely are not referring to actual groups in the church at Rome, it does not rule out Paul's use of variations of diatribe in letters to churches with which he was more familiar.[33] Furthermore, when one takes into account not only the intimate nature of Paul's relationship with the Corinthian church, but also the frequent interchanges between Paul and the congregation, it is almost unimaginable that the apostle would not include allusions to his prior interaction and reflection upon the current thinking of the Corinthians as he wrote his letter.

In 1 Corinthians, Paul is far more aware of the current positions held by those within the church at Corinth than he was with the church in Rome thanks to his ongoing dialogue with the Corinthian Christians via oral reports and letters. And it would be natural for Paul to utilize the rhetorical tools at his disposal to correct the false thinking he had been made aware of in Corinth. Diatribe represented an ideal tool for engaging the various factions within the church. As Stowers points out, in diatribe there are instances where "real objections from the audience seem to occur."[34] Hays notes that this seems to be the case in 1 Corinthians where, although Paul develops an "imaginary dialogue between himself and his Corinthian hearers," the voices to which Paul responds in the conversation represent real slogans or positions of the Corinthian community.[35] Thus, diatribal

---

32. Aune, *The Westminster Dictionary*, 129.

33. Watson agrees, noting that "teaching through diatribe does not preclude addressing a concrete situation" (Watson, "Diatribe," 214).

34. Stowers, *The Diatribe and Paul's Letter to the Romans*, 128.

35. Hays, 101.

rhetoric in the Corinthian correspondence likely reflects, at least at times, a dialogue between Paul and actual Corinthian interlocutors.[36]

Diatribe in 1 Corinthians

While Paul clearly utilizes more of the general characteristics associated with diatribe in Romans than elsewhere, the same rhetorical features are apparent at various places in his other letters as well. For example, in 1 Cor 15:29–35, Paul includes several features associated with diatribe: "rhetorical questions, direct address and exhortation to the audience, a proverbial saying, a quotation from the poet Menander, a question from an imaginary objector, censorious address to the objector, and a comparison."[37] Although we do not find such extensive use of features associated with diatribe in the rest of 1 Corinthians, we do find clear features of diatribal rhetoric. Stowers notes that authors who utilize diatribe often create an imaginary discussion partner who frequently poses absurd conclusions that the teacher/writer then strongly rejects. It is perfectly consistent with diatribe style to have the discussion partner presented in the form of slogans that succinctly capture an actual interlocutor's positions.[38] And this technique appears to occur frequently in 1 Corinthians. Biblical authors regularly used diatribe to move from point to point in their argument "often in the course of disputing the opposing views of others,"[39] and such a strategy, with some variation, is readily apparent in 1 Corinthians, as we will see.[40] The form of diatribe that

---

36. Burk ("Discerning Corinthian Slogans," 10) argues that in 1 Cor 6:12–20 that Paul replaces the normal imaginary dialogue partners with real partners who represent the actual voices within the Corinthian community. Again, we will maintain that if Paul utilized this adaptive type of diatribe in 6:12–20, he would have likely continued the reference to real positions throughout his letter to the Corinthians.

37. Stowers, "The Diatribe," 81.

38. Ibid.

39. Porter, "Diatribe," 298. "The striking characteristic, then, of the phenomenon of objections and false conclusion is the looseness and variability of their usage . . . the author jumps back and forth between dialogue with the imaginary person, direct contact and address to his audience and rhetorical dialogue with himself" (Stowers, *The Diatribe and Paul's Letter to the Romans*, 129).

40. This is common in ancient diatribe. Examples of philosophers citing the opinion of a pupil only to immediately counter it are found in Bion of Borysthenes (third cent. BCE) and Teles of Megara (third cent. BCE); see Schenkeveld, "Diatribe and Dialexis," 232–35. The diatribes of Epictetus (ca. 55–135 CE) provide a more argumentative style of engaging imaginary opponents; ibid., 240–43. The diatribes of Plutarch (ca. 45–120 CE),

seems to be closest to Paul's rhetoric in 1 Corinthians involves his use of a variation of typical diatribal "objections and false conclusions," where the writer records false statements made by his real or imaginary opponent(s) in order to set up his correction of their inaccurate positions.[41] The false statements—in 1 Corinthians typically presented as slogans—essentially serve as literary foils for communicating the author's position.

Summary

Based on our short survey of ancient diatribe, several points are important to keep in mind as we move into our study of 1 Corinthians. First, diatribe was a form of rhetoric by which a philosopher or teacher anticipated objections to his teaching and sought to correct those he was addressing. Second, Paul was clearly familiar with this form of rhetoric as we can see especially from Romans. Third, we know that Paul was intimately aware of positions, issues, and faulty thinking within the Corinthian church, and it would be natural for him to utilize features of diatribe to address these, as he clearly does in Romans. Fourth, there is strong evidence within 1 Corinthians itself that Paul makes use of diatribe in this letter. Given passages with extensive features of diatribe in 1 Corinthians, it is reasonable to expect that Paul may have utilized diatribe elsewhere in the letter to refute other false positions.

Before moving on to the various Corinthian texts where Paul may have quoted Corinthian slogans or positions, we need to do several things. First, we need to ask what grammatical markers were used in the Greek language during the time period that Paul wrote that will help us identify where he is introducing a quote. Second, we need to look deeper into Paul's use of source material and quotations in his writings. Third, we need to seek to establish firm criteria for identifying his use of slogans or other quotations in 1 Corinthians. All of this will ultimately help us responsibly interpret passages where Paul may be quoting Corinthians.

---

contain "imagined interruptions, rhetorical questions, direct addresses to the audience, and striking word-arrangements" (ibid., 245).

41. Recognizing Paul's use of diatribe in 1 Corinthians leads to an alternative analysis to Hurd's (*The Origin of 1 Corinthians*, 82) attempt to distinguish between Paul's responses to oral reports and his responses to the questions asked in the Corinthian letter based on Paul's tone (i.e., Paul's anger when he must raise issues of which he has heard and his gentler tone when Paul responds to questions asked of him).

4

Quotations in Greek Grammar and in Paul's Letters

How do we determine when an author is quoting another source in ancient Greek literature? In Greek grammar, although there were no quotation marks, there were other clues that writers often used to indicate when they were quoting or alluding to another source. To help illustrate how this was done, consider 1 Cor 14:21:

> "In the law it is written, [ὅτι, *hoti*] 'By people of strange tongues and by the lips of foreigners I will speak to this people; yet even then they will not listen to me,' says the Lord."

The expression, "it is written," is enough on its own to signal the likely presence of some sort of quotation in the context. Indeed, Paul often uses this phrase, or "as it is written," to introduce an Old Testament quotation. The fact that the expression is used here with a clearly identified literary source ("the law") makes the presence of a quotation virtually certain. And when we add the use of the Greek conjunction ὅτι (*hoti*), we know that a quotation will immediately follow.[1] Indeed, when ὅτι (*hoti*) is used to introduce

---

1. Since ὅτι (*hoti*) may also function causally (and thus be translated something like "since," or "because") or recitatively (and be translated something like "that"), the reader must be careful to distinguish between the various uses based on context (Robertson, *A Grammar of the Greek New Testament*, 1058). Note that both usages may even occur in the same sentence, as in John 1:51: "Jesus answered and said to him, [ὅτι, *hoti*] 'I said to you that [ὅτι, *hoti*] I saw you under the fig tree'"; author's translation). The first ὅτι (*hoti*) introduces a quote and is thus translated into English using quotation marks; the second one introduces indirect discourse and is thus translated "that."

direct speech it is "practically equivalent to our quotation marks."[2] And since what follows in the previous example can be readily identified as a direct quotation from the Old Testament (Isa 28:11–12), English translations rightly make use of quotation marks here.

As a rule, direct quotes, also known as direct discourse, are typically introduced with a verb of speech, often followed by a ὅτι (*hoti*).[3] What is unusual in 1 Cor 14:21, though, is that the Old Testament quotation is actually a quotation itself of direct speech, as the use of a second verb of speech at the end of the verse ("says the Lord") makes clear.[4] What is the lesson here? The lesson is that one of our first courses of action in seeking to identify quotes within the biblical text is to look for a verb of speech. The verb that introduces a quotation, however, need not be a verb of speech; it may come from the category of "verbs of perception," which includes verbs of thinking, believing, knowing, seeing, and hearing.[5]

It is also important to recognize, however, that the introduction of direct discourse did not require the use of a ὅτι (*hoti*). In fact, direct discourse without a preceding ὅτι (*hoti*) occurs quite frequently, sometimes leading to ambiguity regarding whether or not a quotation is involved.[6] Both direct and indirect discourse are sometimes only indicated by a sud-

---

2. Moulton and Milligan, *The Vocabulary of the Greek New Testament*, 463.

3. This use of the conjunction is often referred to as ὅτι (*hoti*) *recitativum* or recitative ὅτι (*hoti*).

4. Another clue that we can see here is that the grammatical person of the embedded verb will be different from the grammatical person of the preceding part of the passage. In this example, "it is written" (γέγραπται, *gegraptai*) is third person singular, while "I will speak" (λαλήσω, *lalēsō*) is first person singular.

5. Cf. Wallace, *Greek Grammar Beyond the Basics*, 456. Sim actually notes that "the bulk of the examples of ὅτι [*hoti*] in indirect speech refer to a mental representation of the thought of the subject" (Sim, *Marking Thought and Talk*, 156).

6. Interestingly, in the Synoptic tradition, we find that sometimes one version of a saying will include a ὅτι (*hoti*) clause, and another version will not (e.g., Matt 19:19 and Mark 10:11) (Robertson, *A Grammar of the Greek New Testament*, 1028). Levinsohn has argued that a writer's choice as to whether to use ὅτι (*hoti*) to introduce a direct quote or not may have been driven by broader discourse considerations. He suggests that, at least in Luke–Acts and John, "ὅτι *recitativum* is typically used to signal that the speech concerned culminates some unit or at least expands on some previous point" (Levinsohn, *Discourse Features*, 261). Levinsohn goes on to maintain that "ὅτι *recitativum* is used consistently in Luke–Acts and John to signal that the quotation it introduces culminates the argument" (ibid., 269). The fact that when Paul quotes the Corinthians he typically does so to *introduce* a new topic in his argument or refers to Corinthian slogans mid-argument may well explain why we do not typically find a ὅτι (*hoti*) with Corinthian slogans in 1 Corinthians.

den shift in tense that does not seem to fit the flow of a passage, with the writer maintaining the tense found in the quote rather than adjusting it to fit his argument.[7] In 1 Cor 6:16, for example, we encounter an abrupt shift from present tense ("*is* said") to future tense "*shall* be": "Do you not know that whoever is united to a prostitute becomes one body with her? For it is said, 'The two shall be one flesh.'"

Indirect discourse—when an author indirectly reports the words or thoughts of another— is more commonly introduced by a ὅτι (*hoti*) following a verb of speech or perception, often in a clause that uses an infinitive verb. In such cases, the ὅτι (*hoti*) is translated "that." It is important to recognize that often when a writer introduces indirect discourse he is not so much relating exact words, but rather a summary of what someone else has said or summarizing their position. Unfortunately, there are times when there is no way to determine whether a writer is intending to convey direct or indirect discourse, but this rarely affects the interpretation of the text.[8]

Sometimes, the interpreter will only have a change in mood or tone between two statements as a clue that the author is shifting to a quote from another source. At other times, it is only through noticing a contradiction between what the author has been arguing and a new statement that one can determine when he or she is quoting another source. In such cases, the basis for identifying a quotation is not grammatical, but contextual. This means that much skill is required to determine where such quotes are intended by the author.

As we will see in 1 Corinthians, commonly accepted quotes (e.g., 1:12; 7:1; 14:21, 25) follow standard rules of Greek grammar, and so there is little controversy. Possible quotes that are disputed among scholars tend not to follow these rules, which is why they are subject to debate. This is where the study of historical background, rhetoric, textual criticism, apparent contradictions within Paul's argument, and Paul's use of similar phrases elsewhere comes into play. Care must always be taken since the "dangerous

---

7. Dana and Mantey, *A Manual Grammar*, 296; Blass, Debrunner, and Funk, *A Greek Grammar*, §324. Blass, Debrunner, and Funk point us to John 6:24 (εἶδεν ὁ ὄχλος ὅτι Ἰησοῦς οὐκ ἔστιν ἐκεῖ, *eiden ho ochlos hoti Iēsous ouk estin ekei*), where the present tense is used ("Jesus *is* not there") when English would use the past tense ("Jesus *was* not there").

8. Wallace, *Greek Grammar Beyond the Basics*, 457. Levinsohn (*Discourse Features*, 262) suggests that when a writer chooses indirect discourse over direct discourse, he uses it "to *background* the speech with respect to what follows."

subjectivity of locating citations in Pauline letters"[9] can change the way the letters are read both theologically and practically. As we will see, however, a good understanding of context, grammar, and rhetoric can help us gain confidence in identifying where Paul is quoting Corinthians.

Determining When Paul Is Quoting Other Sources

Another problem the interpreter or translator faces is that at times ancient authors quote other sources without giving any indication for their readers that they are referring to what someone else has said.[10] "Paul routinely cited preexisting material—whether an Old Testament text, a saying of Jesus, a line from a Greek poet, an early creedal fragment or hymn, or presumably a Corinthian slogan—without giving explicit indication that he was doing so."[11] While Paul's readers may have recognized the subtle clues that indicate Paul was quoting an outside source, these clues tend to elude modern readers and translators.[12]

Obviously, it would have been very helpful if Paul would have consistently provided an introductory formula to point out when he was about to quote the Corinthians as he did in 1:12 ("What I mean is that each of you says . . .") and 15:12 ("how can some of you say . . ."). The reality is that Paul rarely provides such explicit indications that he is introducing a quote elsewhere. Consider some of his Old Testament quotations in 1 Corinthians alone. In 2:16, he quotes Isa 40:13; in 5:13, he quotes Deut 17:7; in 10:26, he quotes Ps 24:1; in 15:27, he quotes Ps 8:6; and in 15:32, he quotes Isa 22:13. Yet in *none* of these passages does Paul introduce the quotation with any explicit indication that what follows is a quote. Similarly, in 15:33, Paul quotes a popular proverb, "Bad company ruins good morals," which has been confidently traced to the Greek comic poet Menander (fourth century BCE), with no indication that he is quoting another source.[13] A similar type of reference is made in 4:6, where Paul refers to a maxim without provid-

---

9. Willis, *Idol Meat in Corinth*, 97.

10. See Richards, *Paul and First-Century Letter Writing*, 94–95. See also Ramsaran, *Liberating Words*, 3, 22.

11. Smith, "Slogans in 1 Corinthians," 72.

12. Burk ("Discerning Corinthian Slogans," 105–12) argues that Paul's use of a special adaptation of the diatribal form is the clue in 1 Cor 6:12–20 to signal the presence of quoted material.

13. Most English translations use quotation marks here.

ing any explanation that he is quoting someone else's thinking, let alone indicating the source of the adage.[14]

These examples clearly indicate that there are indisputable places in 1 Corinthians where Paul quotes others without specifying the source or providing any indication that he is even quoting someone else. We should, therefore, not expect to find introductory formulas or other explicit indicators each time Paul quotes the Corinthians, especially since he would have expected his readers to be even more familiar with sayings or positions that came from their own community than with material from maxims, Greek poetry, the Old Testament, and so forth. This failure to indicate when a quotation is being introduced, although looked down upon today as plagiarism, would not have been frowned upon in Paul's day. Perspectives toward intellectual property were quite different and "we must not unfairly apply our modern concepts and standards back on Paul."[15] Unfortunately, Paul's "failure" to cite his sources, or at times even provide obvious indicators that a quotation is in view, certainly makes identifying Corinthian quotations in Paul's letter much more complex for the modern reader. And that, in turn, complicates the interpretation of this important letter.

Summary

Now that we are almost ready to begin examining the texts where possible quotations are used, we need to take an inventory of the points we have established so far in our study as we prepare to set forth criteria for evaluating potential slogans or quotations.

1. The apostle Paul had a close relationship with the church he had established in Corinth, a relationship that continued to develop after he left Corinth and that is reflected in his correspondence with them (both oral and written).

2. Through that correspondence, Paul became aware of issues that were threatening the unity and health of the community.

3. Paul's correspondence shows that the Corinthians, at times, operated based on faulty thinking, and Paul saw the need to refute and correct that thinking.

---

14. Some translations provide quotations marks here (NRSV, NIV), while others do not (NASB).

15. Ramsaran, *Liberating Words*, 94.

4. Paul's refutations are found throughout 1 Corinthians, which should be viewed as a "deliberative letter" that deals with issues dividing the church and seeks to persuade them to become united.

5. Paul freely made use of various rhetorical strategies to craft a compelling argument. In particular, he uses elements of diatribe, introducing false conclusions, claims, and positions held by various groups within the church before refuting or correcting them.

6. Since diatribe implies dialogue, and since Paul was in dialogue with real people facing real issues, it would have been natural for Paul to make use of diatribe in 1 Corinthians.

7. Based on the highly occasional nature of Paul's correspondence with the church, it is reasonable that Paul would quote positions of the Corinthians before offering his corrections. Like other ancient authors, however, Paul did not always indicate when he was citing outside sources.

8. The lack of acknowledgment of source material, the lack of quotation marks in ancient Greek, and the lack of explicit grammatical markers can make identifying Corinthian slogans more challenging for the modern reader.

9. Modern scholars do not agree on when Paul was quoting his opponents.

10. Objective criteria are needed for identifying quotes with as much accuracy as possible. Establishing such objective criteria is the last piece of the puzzle before we can begin looking at possible Corinthian quotes in the letter.

5

Reconstructing Corinthian Slogans and Quotations

The evidence we have investigated above suggests that Paul likely utilized a series of slogans and perhaps other quotations in his argument that were associated with the various factions in the Corinthian church, stating their flawed positions before introducing his corrective teachings. Such an approach was a common tactic in ancient Hellenistic rhetoric in which a philosopher or teacher responded to real or anticipated misunderstandings. There is significant scholarly consensus regarding the existence of Corinthians slogans in Paul's letter, but widespread agreement on where quotations occur and where possible quotes begin and end is still lacking. The most comprehensive list is provided by Omanson, who proposes that the following 19 passages contain quotations or Corinthian slogans: 2:15–16a; 4:4; 6:13; 6:18; 7:1; 7:26; 7:34; 8:1; 8:4; 8:8a; 8:9; 8:10; 10:23; 10:29–30; 11:2; 14:21–22; 14:33b–35; and 15:12b.[1] Additional slogans have been posited by a number of scholars, demonstrating the lack of consensus and the need for clear criteria for identifying where Paul is quoting Corinthians.[2]

---

1. Omanson notes that "some of these verses or parts of verses (for instance, 1 Cor 6:12–13) are translated as quotations in most modern translations. Other verses such as 1 Cor 7:1 are treated as quotations by a smaller number of translations. And some verses (for example, 1 Cor 7:26; 14:33–35) are almost never translated as quotations, even though a number of biblical scholars argue that they too are quotations" "Acknowledging Paul's Quotations," 212–13.

2. For example, Siebenmann examines seventeen possible Corinthian slogans, concluding that eight are likely legitimate quotes. His list of potential slogans differs somewhat from the list provided by Omanson (e.g., Siebenmann includes 12:31, but excludes

Reconstructing Corinthian Slogans and Quotations

Establishing Criteria for Identifying Corinthian Slogans

Before we look at the potential slogans themselves, we must ask if it is possible to establish objective criteria for determining when Paul is quoting Corinthians. If an objective set of criteria is not possible, at the very least, we must establish criteria that can be used to weigh the relative merit of reading certain passages as Corinthian slogans or quotations. As we have already seen, several challenges exist for establishing such criteria. First, there is no consistent equivalent of English quotation marks in Koine Greek to allow us to definitively identify quotations. Second, there is no consistent grammatical method used in Koine Greek for citing a source. And third, there is no question that Paul regularly cites outside sources without indicating that he is doing so. Given these realities, we are left to "read between the lines," as it were, drawing on sound exegetical methods in our effort to ascertain when and where Paul is quoting Corinthians. The fact that we are only seeing one side of the conversation compounds the challenges, since Paul would have assumed that the Corinthians would readily spot when their own positions or statements were being referred to even without any explicit markers. How, then, are we to proceed?

Scholars have suggested a number of criteria for detecting slogans:

1. Identify where statements are introduced in an unusual manner.
2. Identify statements that are repeated in the letter.
3. Identify abnormal Pauline vocabulary.
4. Identify superficial contradictions between statements within a single letter.[3]

These suggestions, although limited, provide a helpful starting point. Some of them, however, will be very difficult for students (or even scholars) to utilize, e.g., identifying abnormal Pauline vocabulary, recognizing what constitutes an unusual manner of introducing a statement, or even identifying superficial contradictions.

8:9–10 and 15:12) ("The Question of Slogans in 1 Corinthians"). Hurd, on the other hand, lists 6:12, 13, 18; 7:1, 26; 8:1, 4, 5–6, 8; 10:22; 11:2 as potential Corinthian slogans, which he accepts as legitimate with the exception of 8:5–6 and 8:8 (*The Origin of 1 Corinthians*, 67). Finally, Murphy O'Connor acknowledges that ten passages contain bona fide slogans: 6:12, 13, 18; 7:1; 8:1, 4, 8; 10:23; 11:2; 15:29 (*Key to Corinthians*, 266n41).

3. See Omanson, "Acknowledging Paul's Quotations," 203; Conzelmann, 108–9, 140.

Smith discusses a number of ways that the problem could be approached:[4]

1. Start by examining the characteristics found in the "universally recognized slogans" of 1 Corinthians to establish standards for identifying other possible slogans.[5]
2. Use common sense by noting syntactic irregularities, non-Pauline language, etc.[6]
3. Examine the wider Greco-Roman literature, such as rhetorical handbooks, for any standard approaches.[7]
4. Read the text contextually, "utilizing all possible resources: argument of the passage or flow of thought, idiosyncratic vocabulary and syntax, historical-cultural backgrounds, and so forth," looking for clues that Paul is quoting Corinthians.[8]
5. Observe how the wider interpretative community has viewed the text over time.[9]

Again, these guidelines are very helpful, particularly #2–4, and Smith's work represents a giant step forward.[10] What we believe is needed is more specific guidance for students of Scripture. We would, therefore, suggest twelve clear steps that we can follow to determine with relative confidence when a biblical writer is quoting someone else. To a large degree, these

---

4. Smith, "Slogans in 1 Corinthians," 74, 76–77.

5. Smith (ibid., 74) acknowledges the underlying problem here is that there are essentially no verses in 1 Corinthians that are universally accepted as Corinthian slogans.

6. The weakness of this suggestion lies in the lack of objectivity with which many interpreters often note any "irregularities" in the text.

7. Smith ("Slogans in 1 Corinthians," 75), however, acknowledges the occasional nature of Paul's letters and his unique approach that often fails to follow any standard criteria discussed by the rhetoricians.

8. Ibid., 76n29.

9. It should be noted that, for the most part, it has only been within the last few decades that translators and commentators have begun to recognize that some Pauline passages contain quotations.

10. We do not agree, however, with Smith's contention ("Slogans in 1 Corinthians," 75) that reading 1 Corinthians against the rhetorical handbooks is like comparing apples and oranges given the relatively unique nature of Pauline documents. Paul did not write in a rhetorical vacuum. Like any writer from any age he made the most of the rhetorical conventions of his day to communicate with others in a manner that they would understand.

twelve steps simply represent a fleshing out of Smith's criteria.[11] To help establish a step-by-step process that students can utilize, we will state our criteria in the form of questions. We will also use 1 Cor 1:12 to illustrate how many of the various steps apply.

> "For it has been reported to me by Chloe's people that there are quarrels among you, my brothers and sisters. 12 What I mean is that each of you says, 'I belong to Paul,' or 'I belong to Apollos,' or 'I belong to Cephas,' or 'I belong to Christ.'" (1:11–12)

Identifying Quotations in the New Testament: A Twelve-Step Program

1. *Context: Does the context lead us to expect a quotation?* Yes. In 1:11 Paul refers to a report from Chloe's people (1:10), leading us to expect that portions of that report may follow.

2. *Quotative Frame: Is there a "quotative frame"*[12] *in the near context?* Yes. 1 Cor 1:12 includes "each of you *says,*" immediately preceding the potential quotes. Although Greek does not use quotation marks, it does use quotative frames, such as "he said," to indicate that a quotation will follow. These will be the surest mark that a quote is in view, but we must remember that quotative frames will frequently not be used with slogans. Sometimes the quotative frame will include a ὅτι (*hoti*) immediately preceding the potential quote, and this provides strong additional evidence for a quotation; but this is not typically the case in 1 Corinthians.

3. *Shift in Person: Is there a shift in grammatical "person" (first person, second person, third person)?* Yes. 1 Cor 1:12 moves from *"you* say" to *"I* belong."

4. *Proverbial Statements: Is there a potential slogan in the form of generalizations, like a proverbial statement (usually expressed in the present tense)?* No. A good example of such a statement in 1 Corinthians is "all things are lawful" (6:12).

5. *Rhetorical Features: Are there rhetorical features, such as parallel structures, that might suggest an easy to memorize catchphrase (slogan)?* No. A good example of this is 6:13: "Food is meant for the stomach and

---

11. See Smith, "Slogans in 1 Corinthians," 84–86.
12. See Runge, *Discourse Grammar*, 145.

the stomach for food." Notice the food-stomach-stomach-food word order here.

6. *Repetition: Are there expressions that are repeated at other points in the letter?* Yes and No. In 1 Cor 1:12, there are expressions that are actually repeated four times in a single verse ("I belong to . . . ," lit. "I am of . . ."), though not in the remainder of the letter.

7. *Diatribe: Are features of diatribe present or other rhetorical features that may suggest the presence of dialogue between the writer and others?* Yes. In 1 Cor 1:12, Paul writes (literally), "*I* am saying this, because each of *you* is saying…" (our translation).

8. *Contradictions: Are there statements that appear to contradict what the author says elsewhere in the same letter?* No, not in 1:12. A good example of this phenomenon is 7:1 ("it is good for a man not to touch a woman"), which appears to contradict the high value Paul places on sexual relations within marriage in the same context (7:2–5).

9. *Contrast: Does the writer present a sharp contrast or refutation to something he has just stated, which may have been a quotation? Or, does he make a statement and then provide commentary on that statement as if referring to something that has been expressed by others?*[13] Yes. There is a strong refutation in 1:13.

10. *Common Issues: Are there expressions that may represent characteristic ways of thinking, based on the broad context of the letter, that the writer appears to be engaging with his audience?* Yes. Paul has just referred to "divisions" in 1:10, and placing the multiple cases of "I belong to . . . " in the mouths of the Corinthians fits with that context.

As we have seen, evidence for slogans in 1 Cor 1:12 is extremely strong. To finish our analysis of this and other passages we must also consider how earlier scholars and English Bible translations have handled the passage, and whether our analysis passes the common sense test. In order to answer questions 11–12, we will consider a representative sample of ten

---

13. This is also the case, for example, with 2:16, where Paul quotes from Isa 40:13 without explicitly introducing it as a quotation. He does, however, proceed to springboard off that statement with commentary of his own: "But we have the mind of Christ." If this study were concerned with identifying Old Testament quotes in addition to quotes from the writer's addressees, we would add the criteria: Does the writer introduce a statement and then proceed to offer commentary on it as if the statement comes from an outside source? Can that material be located in the Old Testament?

Reconstructing Corinthian Slogans and Quotations

English Bible translations[14] and fifteen commentators[15] for each passage.[16] In the following chapters we will then systematically apply our twelve step program to help us identify Corinthian slogans or other quotations in ten additional passages: 6:12; 6:13–14; 6:18; 7:1; 8:1; 8:4; 8:8; 10:23; 14:21–25; and 14:33b-35. Readers will then be well-equipped to apply these same principles to other New Testament texts on their own.

> 11–12. *Past Scholars and Common Sense: Is our assessment of a particular putative slogan consistent with the collective wisdom of Bible scholars and Bible translators? Does our assessment of a particular putative slogan pass the common sense test (i.e., does reading a particular text as a slogan or quotation make the best sense of the immediate context)?* Yes. Almost all scholars and English versions believe there are quotations in 1:12.[17]

All of the Bible translations under consideration make use of quotation marks in 1:12 to indicate that the claims of allegiance were Corinthian positions that Paul was citing. Not all of the commentators we are considering, however, agree that there are slogans or quotations in view here. Nine of the fifteen appear to interpret Paul as quoting Corinthian slogans. Talbert acknowledges that Chloe's people have reported to Paul that the Corinthians are quarreling about ministers by giving their spiritual guides too much status, and this is bringing dissention within the body.[18] Keener adds that "Political parties were named for the founders to which adherents professed loyalty, and slogans analogous to, 'I am of so-and-so'

---

14. New Revised Standard Version (NRSV), New American Standard Bible (NASB), New King James Version (NKJV), New International Version (NIV 1984 and NIV 2011), the NET Bible (NET), English Standard Version (ESV), New Jerusalem Bible (NJB), Modern English Version (MEV), and the Holman Christian Standard Bible (HCSB). Since the KJV does not use quotation marks at all, it was not relevant for our study.

15. We will examine the major commentaries by C. K. Barrett, Craig Blomberg, Hans Conzelmann, F. F. Bruce, Gordon D. Fee, Joseph A. Fitzmyer, David E. Garland, Richard B. Hays, Craig S. Keener, Charles Talbert, Anthony Thiselton, Ben Witherington, Roy E. Ciampa and Brian S. Rosner, Timothy A. Brookins and Bruce W. Longecker, and Mark Taylor. These are cited in footnotes throughout using page numbers only.

16. We will not attempt to summarize the view of every commentator for every passage.

17. For more on the individual parties themselves, see Conzelmann, 33–34; Thiselton, 123–34.

18. Talbert, 4.

characterized rivalries of political, academic, and athletic factions."[19] Hays indicates that "these slogans have probably arisen spontaneously within the Corinthian church," and Paul sees the need to stamp out these unneeded distractions.[20] Fee notes that when Paul says that "each one of you is saying," he probably "does not mean that every individual is involved in the sloganeering, but that the whole church has been affected by it. The slogan literally reads 'I am of (Paul),' which means something like 'I am Paul's person,' or as the NIV has it, 'I follow Paul.'"[21]

Witherington, Blomberg, Fitzmyer, Taylor, Brookins/Longenecker, and perhaps Conzelmann, on the other hand, maintain that while Paul was dealing with actual Corinthian behaviors that were causing division within the church, he was not necessarily addressing literal set slogans by the parties involved. Fitzmyer points out that "when Paul speaks of 'each one,' he rhetorically expresses the individuality and divisive character of the situation in Corinth and not a real slogan since it could merely be Paul's way of verbalizing an allegiance.[22] Witherington, Blomberg, and Brookins/Longenecker likewise merely see Paul using rhetorical tools here, rather than actual Corinthian slogans, to refute their divisive behaviors. Taylor, however, notes that "Even if the slogans are caricatures created by Paul, his rhetorical flourish works precisely because it accurately sheds light on the true situation."[23] Paul is no doubt referring to positions of personal preference that were causing division within the body; and he makes use of clear refutation language that draws on features of diatribe.[24]

Likelihood of a Quotation in 1:12: *Very Likely.*

19. Keener, 24.

20. Hays, 22.

21. Fee, 56. Barrett (43) notes that "The existence of a 'Paul-group' itself implies opposition to Paul in Corinth." Garland (50) adds that "there were good reasons for Paul not to attack the party leaders directly. For one thing, his information about the division came to him by hearsay from Chloe's household. To name names on hearsay evidence can cause trouble not only for the namer, but also for the informants."

22. Fitzmyer, 142.

23. Taylor, 56–57.

24. Remember, as we noted above, when Paul "quotes" the Corinthians he may be putting their thinking or behavior into a succinct statement that he has *himself* created as a convenient way of engaging their position. As Mitchell notes, "While the Corinthians themselves may not have expressed their allegiance in this fashion, Paul interprets their factional activity as indicative, not of political sophistication, but of childishness and renunciation of their precious freedom through their alignment behind various missionaries" (Mitchell, *Paul and the Rhetoric of Reconciliation*, 86).

Theological Implications

So what? What are the theological implications of acknowledging the presence of slogans or quotations in 1:12? Recognizing that Paul is quoting Corinthians sets us up for Paul's response to the Corinthian positions. Paul emphatically rebukes the factionalism in Corinth by means of three rhetorical questions in verse 13, each of which is stated in such a way that it demands a negative answer: "Has Christ been divided? Was Paul crucified for you? Or were you baptized in the name of Paul?" Paul quotes the Corinthians, then, so that he can reinforce their common loyalty to the one Christ and highlight the folly of using loyalty to human leaders (or a divisive claim of loyalty to Christ) to bolster their own status.[25]

The Corinthians were actually a lot like many of us. North Americans love to be associated with "their team." When the team we cheer for wins the Super Bowl, we scream, "*We* won!" When a particular basketball team makes the playoffs, we say, "*We* made it!" Why? We actually had nothing whatsoever to do with the team's success, but it makes us feel good to be connected to a winner. The Corinthians were no different,[26] only their heroes were those who could speak like a philosopher. Eloquence and wisdom were the badges of greatness in their day, and association with individuals who possessed these qualities allowed the Corinthians to feel proud, and, more importantly, to gain honor in the community. Paul reminds them that this is worldly thinking that is inconsistent with God's way of doing things. Followers of Christ are to have lives that center around glorifying God through serving the Lord Jesus Christ. And they must even be on guard so that their devotion to serving Christ not be tainted by selfish ambition, as Paul's reference to the "I am of Christ" faction makes clear.

Finally, it is important to note that this first rebuke of Corinthian positions sets the tone for the rest of the refutations that will follow. Paul does not sugarcoat his corrections. The Corinthians have serious problems, and Paul intends to draw them to their attention. In this case, he does so by

---

25. See Garland, 49.

26. Witherington (11) notes that "by the end of the first century a.d. Roman Corinth had acquired a reputation for being the most competitive of all cities, even in economic matters." For the Corinthians, this type of thinking was an even bigger problem than today, since they were not only competitive (as we are) but used competitions of all sorts as means of gaining status.

highlighting the absurdity of their thinking. This implicitly raises the question, "Where else have we gone wrong?" and thus prepares the Corinthians for the reproof and reprimands that will follow.

6

The Corinthians and Sexuality

Libertinism

The first set of slogans that we saw in 1:12 might be called slogans about unity (or disunity!). Paul took up the Corinthians' own words as a rhetorical tool for demolishing their highly destructive ways of thinking. Ultimately, these slogans point to people who were followers of Jesus but who had brought the broader culture's pursuit of individual honor and status into the church. Much of what we see in the subsequent chapters flows out of this same selfish ambition, with Paul appealing to the Corinthians to get their focus off themselves and onto the glory of God and the edification of the church, of which they are all a part. The closely intertwined issues of disunity, factionalism, and individual pursuit of honor represent the overarching problem that was plaguing the Corinthian church in the first century. But Paul also addresses specific issues within the church, and he appears to refer to slogans (or other types of Corinthian quotations) as he does so, just as he did in 1:12. As we consider ten other passages in 1 Corinthians for evidence of slogans or quotations, we will organize our discussion around what the Corinthians were saying about sexuality, community, and order. We begin with passages that make use of apparent slogans relating to sexuality. More specifically, this chapter will focus on slogans that reveal a libertine attitude toward sexuality ("anything goes"), while the next chapter will deal with the superficially opposite view toward sexuality (asceticism).

1 Corinthians 6:12–20

Omanson points out that "Chapter 6 of 1 Corinthians is the one chapter where there is most agreement among modern commentators and translators that Paul is citing phrases that come from the Corinthians themselves."[1] First Corinthians 6:12–20 contains four possible Corinthian slogans quoted by the apostle that he then proceeds to refute and correct.[2] One potential slogan is repeated twice in rapid succession in a single verse:

> "'All things are lawful for me,' but not all things are beneficial. 'All things are lawful for me,' but I will not be dominated by anything." (6:12)

The other two possible slogans are built around a misunderstanding that would disconnect acts of sin in the present life with one's new existence in the age to come:

> "'Food is meant for the stomach and the stomach for food,' and God will destroy both one and the other. The body is meant not for fornication but for the Lord, and the Lord for the body." (6:13)

> "Shun fornication! Every sin that a person commits is outside the body; but the fornicator sins against the body itself." (6:18)

Careful readers will notice that there are no indications in the NRSV of a quotation in 6:18. We will examine the evidence relating to that passage below. We begin, though, by applying our twelve steps to 1 Cor 6:12. As we saw above, the NRSV uses quotation marks to indicate the translation committee's assumption that Paul is quoting the Corinthians at two points in this verse. How strong is the evidence for this view?

---

1. Omanson, "Acknowledging Paul's Quotations," 204.

2. Blomberg (125) notes the typical pattern in Paul's use of slogans: Paul begins by "quoting a Corinthian slogan, and thereby giving it a limited endorsement, but then at once substantially qualifies it. These Corinthian slogans (here the three sayings of verses 12–13 which the NIV encloses with quotation marks) all share four characteristics: (a) they are short, pithy, and proverbial; (b) they reflect the libertine wing of the church; (c) Paul himself could have conceivably uttered them in some specific context; and (d) apart from that context they were so misleading that abuse was almost inevitable."

Twelve Steps for Identifying Quotations: 1 Cor 6:12

> "'All things are lawful for me,' but not all things are beneficial. 'All things are lawful for me,' but I will not be dominated by anything." (6:12)

1. *Context: Does the context lead us to expect a quotation?* Yes. In 1 Cor 5–7, Paul is clearly confronting various flawed positions within the church that revolve around sexuality and "freedom." We see in 5:1 that it was reported to Paul that a particularly shocking case of sexual immorality was being tolerated by the church in Corinth: "It is actually reported that there is sexual immorality among you, and of a kind that is not found even among pagans; for a man is living with his father's wife." What was the Corinthians' response to this gross sin? They were actually proud of the situation (5:2), and even *boasted* about how enlightened they were to allow such behavior (5:6). Though Paul does not at this point quote what they were saying, his reference to their boasting provides a contextual clue indicating that quotations of the Corinthian positions may occur once again in this section of the letter.

2. *Quotative Frame: Is there a "quotative frame" in the near context?* No.

3. *Shift in Person: Is there a shift in grammatical "person"?* No. Paul continues to use the first person ("for me") in the putative quote.

4. *Proverbial Statements: Is there a potential slogan in the form of a generalization, like a proverbial statement (usually expressed in the present tense)?* Yes. This statement actually closely mirrors a saying that may have been known to the Corinthians from Sirach 37:28a: "Not everything is good for everyone."[3]

5. *Rhetorical Features: Are there rhetorical features, such as parallel structures, that might suggest an easy to memorize catchphrase?* Yes. Paul has without question made use of a parallel structure:

   "All things are lawful for me"
   But not all things are beneficial
   "All things are lawful for me"
   But I will not be dominated by anything

---

3. In Greek, Sirach reads, οὐ . . . πάντα πᾶσιν συμφέρει (*ou panta pasin sumferei*), while Paul writes, οὐ πάντα συμφέρει (*ou panta sumferei*). The only difference is that Paul leaves out "for everyone" (πᾶσιν, *pasin*) to make it fit his argument better. This suggests that Paul is engaging in a game of dueling slogans at this point.

6. *Repetition: Are there expressions that are repeated at other points in the letter?* Yes. The fact that Paul uses the exact same clause twice in the same verse increases the likelihood that he is quoting Corinthians here. The fact that he uses the same statement twice more in quick succession later in the letter (10:23) is powerful evidence for a quotation both here and there.

7. *Diatribe: Are features of diatribe present or other rhetorical features that may suggest the presence of dialogue between the writer and others?* Yes. Although there is no evidence of diatribe preceding v. 12, as we will see below in our discussion of 6:18 there is strong evidence of diatribe in what follows.

8. *Contradictions: Are there statements that appear to contradict what the author says elsewhere in the same letter?* Yes. Paul has just made it clear in 6:9–10 that certain behaviors are utterly incongruent with faith in Jesus Christ. Thus, for him to say himself, "All things are lawful for me," would be a blatant contradiction.

9. *Contrast: Does the writer present a sharp contrast or refutation to something he has just stated, which may have been a quotation? Or, does he make a statement and then provide commentary on that statement as if referring to something that has been expressed by others?* Yes. After each potential quotation, what follows is introduced by the conjunction ἀλλά (*alla*, commonly translated "but"), which is typically used in Greek to introduce a strong contrast. In this particular context, Paul is clearly contrasting what follows the conjunction with what precedes (an alternative view).[4] That contrast is made even more clear by his use of not only the conjunction, but also a negative "but *not*" (ἀλλ' οὐ[κ], *all' ou[k]*). This is readily apparent in most English translations as well.

10. *Common Issues: Are there expressions that may represent characteristic ways of thinking, based on the broad context of the letter, that the writer appears to be engaging with his audience?* Yes. The letter reveals a strong individualistic, self-seeking attitude among the Corinthians.

---

4. As we will see, Paul follows a fairly consistent pattern throughout this letter. He often begins a sub-section by stating a Corinthian positon, and then follows this with his refutation of their position commonly introduced by the adversative conjunction ἀλλά (*alla*) or the conjunction δέ (*de*) (see 6:12a; 6:12b; 6:13; 6:18; 7:1–2; 8:1–2; 8:6–7; 8:8–9; 10:23a; 10:23b).

This is revealed in their sexual pursuits, their willingness to take other believers to court, their commitment to eating food that had been sacrificed to idols regardless of how it impacted fellow believers, and so forth. This "I can do whatever I please" attitude toward life is nicely captured in the saying, "All things are lawful for me."

11–12. *Past Scholars and Common Sense: Is our assessment of a particular putative slogan consistent with the collective wisdom of Bible scholars and Bible translators? Does our assessment of a particular putative slogan pass the common sense test (i.e., does reading a particular text as a slogan or quotation make the best sense of the immediate context)?* Yes. Past scholars and translations strongly support the presence of quotations here. The NRSV, NIV 1984, NIV 2011, NET, ESV, NJB, MEV, and HCSB all identify the phrase, "All things are lawful for me," as a Corinthian quote by enclosing it in quotation marks. Only the NKJV and NASB do not use quotation marks.

The majority of modern scholars likewise believe that Paul was quoting Corinthians here. Among the commentators consulted for this study, only Garland argues that 1 Cor 6:12a and 6:12b do not include Corinthian slogans quoted by Paul.[5] He maintains that Paul must not be citing a Corinthian slogan because he has used "for me" in 12a and 12b.[6] He goes on to suggest that "in 6:12, 'for me' appears to have been included to balance the 'I' in the second rebuttal, 'I will not be overmastered by anything.'"[7] Garland also believes that if Paul had been actually quoting a slogan as a license to freely commit sexual sin, he would have been much more direct and forceful in his rebuttal.[8]

Keener takes a different approach. He maintains that quotation marks should be used with the repeated statement since he views the maxim as Paul's anticipation of Corinthian objections, whether or not the Corinthians actually used this maxim themselves.[9] Paul, thus, encapsulates the position he is refuting in the form of a slogan in order to provide general instructions regarding the way Corinthians ought to behave as those who

---

5. Garland, 227–28.
6. Ibid., 28.
7. Ibid.
8. Ibid.
9. Keener, 57.

have devoted their lives to God.[10] In this view, Paul is addressing an anticipated misunderstanding, rather than quoting an actual statement of the Corinthians.

The other scholars we are considering (Hays, Bruce, Barrett, Conzelmann, Fee, Witherington, Blomberg, Talbert, Thiselton, Taylor, Brookins/Longenecker, Ciampa/Rosner, and Fitzmyer) all agree or appear to agree that in both 6:12a and 6:12b Paul is quoting a Corinthian slogan, and that Paul uses something like counter-slogans to begin his rebuttal. Fee, for example, argues that "'Everything is permissible for me' is almost certainly a Corinthian theological slogan. This is confirmed by the way Paul cites it again in 10:23; in both cases he qualifies it so sharply as to negate it—at least as a theological absolute."[11]

Thiselton agrees, noting that his interpretation of the Corinthian slogan, "Liberty to do anything," and Paul's rebuttal, "But I will not let anything take liberties with me," captures "all the appropriate nuances, combining Corinthian triumphalism and sloganizing with Paul's related theology of redefined freedom. It is a well-known paradox that if *everyone* claims unqualified autonomy, *no one* can be free, for everyone is threatened by the freedoms of the other."[12]

In the end, it is impossible to get around the common sense argument that Paul must be quoting Corinthians here because the quotes would contradict his teaching in the rest of the letter and are immediately corrected here. It is not surprising, then, that there is almost universal agreement that Paul is referring to Corinthian claims in this passage.

Likelihood of a Quotation in 6:12: *Very likely.* We will save our discussion of the theological implications of this analysis for our discussion of the full passage (1 Cor 6:12–20) below.

---

10. Ibid.

11. Fee (251–52) adds that "the source of the slogan remains debatable," for it is possible that "the Corinthians had turned a Pauline position into a slogan for their own purposes."

12. Thiselton, 461.

Twelve Steps for Identifying Quotations: 1 Cor 6:13–14

> "'Food is meant for the stomach and the stomach for food,' and God will destroy both one and the other. The body is meant not for fornication but for the Lord, and the Lord for the body. And God raised the Lord and will also raise us by his power." (6:13–14)

When we come to 1 Cor 6:13, we encounter what appears to be another Corinthian slogan. Our task in evaluating this slogan, however, is more complicated than in 6:12. It is not at all clear that Paul is indeed quoting Corinthians here, and if he is where the quote ends. Some extend the quote to the end of the first sentence: "'Food is for the stomach and the stomach is for food, but God will do away with both.' The body is not for sexual immorality, but for the Lord, and the Lord for the body" (NET). So, we will have to test both the shorter and longer quote hypotheses using our twelve steps. We will focus on the shorter quote hypothesis first, and then evaluate the longer quote hypothesis more briefly at the end of our discussion of this passage.

1. *Context: Does the context lead us to expect a quotation?* Yes. To the evidence from context cited above for 6:12 we can add that we now also have strong evidence that Paul has just quoted Corinthians in the previous verse, repeating the same slogan twice. This sets our expectation higher that there may be more quotations to follow.
2. *Quotative Frame: Is there a "quotative frame" in the near context?* No.
3. *Shift in Person: Is there a shift in grammatical "person"?* Yes. Paul has just said, "I will not be dominated by anything." He now shifts to third person.
4. *Proverbial Statements: Is there a potential slogan in the form of a generalization, like a proverbial statement (usually expressed in the present tense)?* Yes.
5. *Rhetorical Features: Are there rhetorical features, such as parallel structures, that might suggest an easy to memorize catchphrase?* Yes. There is a clear food-stomach-stomach-food structure.
6. *Repetition: Are there expressions that are repeated at other points in the letter?* No.
7. *Diatribe: Are features of diatribe present or other rhetorical features that may suggest the presence of dialogue between the writer and others?* Yes.

Not only do we have the very strong likelihood that Paul has just cited and then refuted Corinthian quotes in verse 12, explicitly dialoguing with their position, as we will see below there is also strong evidence of diatribe in what follows.

8. *Contradictions: Are there statements that appear to contradict what the author says elsewhere in the same letter?* Yes. Paul has just stated, "I will not be dominated by anything" (v. 12). To then say that he believes one should indulge in food whenever one wants appears to be a contradiction. Later, he will very strongly rebuke the Corinthians for their eating practices when they gather together, even going so far as to say that God has disciplined them because of these offensive practices by making some of them sick and others die (see 11:17–31).

9. *Contrast: Does the writer present a sharp contrast or refutation to something he has just stated, which may have been a quotation?* No, but he does present a *likely* refutation. Rather than using the conjunction ἀλλά (*alla*, "but"), as in the previous verse, he uses the conjunction δέ (*de*). This conjunction, which is sometimes wrongly referred to as having an adversative function by Greek grammarians, serves to "represent the writer's choice to explicitly signal that what follows is a new development in the story or argument, based on how the writer conceived of it,"[13] or simply to introduce information that is distinctive. When that new development contrasts with what precedes, based on the context, the conjunction is naturally translated "but," even though it does not carry any adversative force on its own.

10. *Common Issues: Are there expressions that may represent characteristic ways of thinking, based on the broad context of the letter, that the writer appears to be engaging with his audience?* Yes. As we noted above, 1 Corinthians reveals a strong individualistic, self-seeking attitude among some of the Christians in Corinth. This "I can do whatever I please" attitude toward life is nicely captured in the saying, "All things are lawful for me." And it is also reflected in the casual approach to gratifying physical urges reflected in the statement "food for the stomach, and the stomach for food"[14] (6:13).

---

13. Runge, *Discourse Grammar*, 31; cf. Dooley and Levinsohn, *Analyzing Discourse*, 93.

14. Our translation, which follows the Greek more closely than the NRSV, makes it clearer how brief and memorable this saying was.

11–12. *Past Scholars and Common Sense: Is our assessment of a particular putative slogan consistent with the collective wisdom of Bible scholars and Bible translators? Does our assessment of a particular putative slogan pass the common sense test (i.e., does reading a particular text as a slogan or quotation make the best sense of the immediate context)?* Yes. The vast majority of English translations explicitly mark 6:13a as a quote, with most ending the quote after "food" (NRSV, NIV 1984, ESV, MEV, HCSB), while some end the quote after "other" (NIV 2011; NET).[15] The NKJB, NASB, and NJB do not use quotation marks in this passage at all.

When we turn to our commentaries, we find that Garland once again sees no slogan in the text.[16] Keener, on the other hand, argues that the assertion, "Food is meant for the stomach and the stomach for food," probably does not represent a specific Corinthian position per se, but rather is to be associated with common Greek logic in general that would seek to justify gluttony.[17] In this view, the text in question is an objection anticipated by Paul and therefore is appropriately placed in quotes.

Blomberg and Conzelmann acknowledge the presence of a slogan in 6:13, but Blomberg is unsure where the quotation ends, and Conzelmann does not address the question of a longer quote.[18] In contrast, ten of our other scholars—Bruce, Barrett, Witherington, Talbert, Thiselton, Hays, Fee, Ciampa/Rosner, Brookins/Longenecker, and Fitzmyer[19]—argue that the Corinthian slogan in 6:13 also includes the words, "and God will destroy both one and the other." Fitzmyer notes that while some interpreters end the quote after "food," "the relationship expressed in the last part of v. 13 and v. 14 and especially the parallelism between v. 13a and v. 13b" make it clear that the quote should be extended.[20] With Fitzmyer, Talbert argues that the structure of the section helps to reveal that the Corinthian position

---

15. The NRSV points out in a footnote the possibility that the quote could end after "other."

16. See Garland's (225–32) extensive arguments against the use of slogans in 6:12–13.

17. Keener, 57.

18. Blomberg, 126. That portion of the verse was not included as part of the quote by the NIV 1984, but is included in the NIV 2011.

19. Taylor is noncommittal regarding the question of whether a slogan is being quoted here at all.

20. Fitzmyer, 264.

comes as a two-part assertion: "the moral principle (v. 13a, 'Food is meant for the stomach and the stomach for food') and its basis (v. 13b, 'God will destroy both the one and the other')."[21] In this reading, Paul emphatically rejects this line of thinking by arguing against the two-fold Corinthian assertion with a two-fold rebuttal of his own. His first counter argument is also based on a moral principle: "The body is meant not for fornication but for the Lord, and the Lord for the body" (v. 13c). Here, Paul rebukes the assertions made by the Corinthians by arguing that believers' bodies are not to be joined with immorality, but with the Lord.[22] For Talbert, since the word "body" (v. 13) is parallel to the personal pronoun "us" (v. 14), it is intended to indicate that one's entire self, the whole of human life, both physical and spiritual, is intended to be united and submitted to Christ.[23] Talbert goes on to note that this moral principle is followed by the basis upon which it rests: "And God raised the Lord and will also raise us by his power" (v. 14). As Jesus was raised from the dead by God's power (cf. 1 Cor. 15:4, 12), so also believers will be raised (cf. Rom 8:11). Paul has thus, according to Talbert, turned the Corinthian assertion on its head. As they believed that the earthly and physical nature of sexual intercourse proves the neutrality of sexual behavior, Paul asserts that the "bodily resurrection sets the seal to the moral and religious significance of the body. God's act to continue bodily life [through the resurrection] indicates that what is done in the sphere of human life has ultimate meaning."[24]

So, how do these scholarly conclusions and arguments fit with our analysis above? And do they pass the common sense test? Talbert's arguments are certainly compelling, and so are those of Hays and Fee, which we did not examine in detail. We could simply say "majority wins" like good advocates of democracy, but such an approach would be scholarly malpractice. What might a fresh look at this passage reveal?

21. Talbert, 29. Hays and Fee both also point to the parallel structure in 6:12–13 and argue that it strongly suggests that the phrase "and God will destroy both one and the other" is the view of the Corinthians and not that of Paul, since "the idea that the physical body is unimportant is precisely the point that Paul is trying to refute" (Hays, 103).

22. Fitzmyer (265) emphasizes the parallelism of formulation, as originally pointed out by Murphy-O'Connor ("Corinthian Slogans," 394): "As the Corinthian slogan spoke of 'food for the stomach, and the stomach for food,' so Paul retorts, 'the body . . . For the Lord, and the Lord for the body,' making use of chiasmus."

23. Talbert (30) notes that Paul uses the language characteristic with the marriage union here (i.e., "to be for," cf. Song of Sol 2:16; Rom 7:2–3): "The Christian's body is meant not for union with Immorality but for union with the Lord."

24. Ibid.

The Context does not offer us any clues regarding where the quote ends. It merely leads us to have some level of expectation that one or more quotes may be present. There are no Quotative Frames, and even if there were, they would not indicate where the quote ended. There is no Shift in Person. We can say, however, that the short version of the quote ("Food is meant for the stomach and the stomach for food") makes a good Proverbial Statement, while the long version does not, though it could represent two slogans that have been linked together or simply represent an extended Corinthian quotation.[25] We need to pause here, because our English translations make the second half of the putative quotation sound more "quote-like" than the Greek text does. The NRSV translates it "God will destroy both one and the other," which sounds a bit like a proverbial statement. The Greek, however, more strictly reads, "God will destroy both this [stomach] and these [foods]." The use of the demonstratives ("this" and "these") makes it far more likely that this clause is a comment on the preceding clause rather than a part of a slogan or quotation. It also effectively rules out the possibility that Paul is citing two slogans here that he has combined.

In terms of Rhetorical Features, the parallelism we noted above for 6:13a is significantly weakened if we include 6:13b as part of the quotation. Neither the criterion of Repetition nor Diatribe assists us in determining where the quote ends; nor does the criterion of Contradiction. When we look at the question of Contrast, on the other hand, we find some light shed on the question at hand. As we noted above, Paul introduces 6:13b with the conjunction δέ (*de*), marking it as a new development in his argument. While it is possible that the Corinthians could have used δέ (*de*) as part of their slogan, it would have been more likely for them to use a different conjunction if it were part of their slogan.[26] Finally, the emphasis on the coming end of food and our stomachs as we know them could reflect either Paul's or the Corinthians' eschatological sentiments (Common Issues).

In the end, our use of the twelve steps not only leads us to conclude that 6:13 very likely contains a Corinthian slogan, but it also offers some basis for determining where that slogan ends. The proverbial nature that we expect with slogans is preserved with the shorter quote hypothesis, as is the

---

25. An extended Corinthian quotation is less likely given the fact that Paul does not yet appear to be addressing issues that were raised in the Corinthians' letter.

26. The conjunction καί (*kai*) would have been more natural, because it would have marked what follows in 6:13b as a continuation of what they had just said in 6:13a: "Food is for the body and the body for food, *and* (καί, *kai*) God is going to destroy them both anyway."

clear parallel structure, which is lost with the longer quote, especially when we look at the Greek text. What we find in the second part of the putative quotation (Greek:[27] "God will destroy both this and these") clearly does not qualify as a slogan itself. Finally, most scholars have failed to consider the significance of Paul's use of δέ (*de*) in the second clause of 6:13, which most likely marks it as him presenting the next development in his argument, rather than the second half of a Corinthian quote.

When read as a Corinthian slogan, in the first part of 6:13 Paul's opponents seem to be making the case that sexual conduct has no moral or eternal significance, since believers are now "spiritual" and are positioned above the deeds done in the physical realm.[28] The Corinthians were apparently attempting to distance themselves from deeds done in the physical body (especially deeds related to food and sex). At first glance, it may seem difficult to believe that the position found in the second clause of 6:13 could be Paul's view, since the statement appears to indicate a belief that the believer's physical body is destined for destruction, while Paul in the same context (6:14) and later in the letter emphasizes the coming resurrection of the body (1 Cor 15). There need not be any contradiction, however, since Paul here is simply saying that both food and the stomach, as we know them, are for this age only.

Paul clearly goes on to reject dualistic thinking—in this case, a sharp distinction between the physical and the spiritual, which leads to thinking that what is done in the body has no bearing on one's spiritual life—and instead argues that the believer's body does not simply belong to the temporary physical sphere as the Corinthians claim, but instead will be raised from the dead (cf. 6:14; 15:12–58). Therefore, the believer's body is "for the Lord" (6:13), and not for self-indulgence. He also, however, makes it clear that the resurrected body will be quite different from the current body (15:44). Indeed, this body "cannot inherit the kingdom of God" (15:50). In one sense, then, the body we currently inhabit *will* be destroyed . . . the body *as we know it*. Its destruction, however, will come by our current physical body being raised from the dead (highlighting its importance) and then transformed into a new spiritual body, which is still material in nature. In that body, the stomach and its relationship to food will no longer be the

---

27. ὁ δὲ θεὸς καὶ ταύτην καὶ ταῦτα καταργήσει, *ho de theos kai tautēn kai tauta katargēsei*.

28. Thiselton (462) goes on to argue that this slogan gives further support for the slogan in the previous verse, since to be "above" earthly matters coheres with the claim to be "above" the law as spiritual persons.

same (likewise, the body's relationship to sex), but that does not mean that what is done with our bodies in this life is insignificant in God's eyes.

Likelihood of a Quotation in 6:13–14: *Very likely*, with the quote most likely being the shorter version: "Food is meant for the stomach and the stomach for food," following the NRSV and the majority of the English versions we surveyed, while going against the majority of commentaries we examined. Although an extended quotation would make very good sense of 6:13—indeed, it would allow us to quickly resolve the apparent tensions in this verse—acknowledging the presence of Corinthian quotations in this letter must not serve as a license to resort to quotation theories whenever the text as we find it is difficult to interpret. It is critical that we have explicit criteria that point to a quotation, rather than simply relying on what sounds logical to our modern ears. Below, we will introduce some supplemental criteria for evaluating potential extended quotations. The most important of those criteria is that an extended quotation must begin with a quotative frame, which is lacking in 6:13.

Twelve Steps for Identifying Quotations: 1 Cor 6:18

> "Shun fornication! Every sin that a person commits is outside the body; but the fornicator sins against the body itself." (6:18)

First Corinthians 6:18 is a notoriously difficult verse to interpret. What does Paul mean by saying, "Every sin that a person commits is outside the body," and how does it relate to the rest of what he says here? Is this Paul's own claim or a claim that some of the Corinthians were making? Our twelve steps should help us to answer these questions.

1. *Context: Does the context lead us to expect a quotation?* Yes and No. We have already been conditioned to expect quotations in this passage, but there is nothing in the near context to point to a quotation.
2. *Quotative Frame: Is there a "quotative frame" in the near context?* No.
3. *Shift in Person: Is there a shift in grammatical "person"?* Yes. There is a shift from second person ("[You] Shun fornication!") to third person ("Every sin"), and then back to second person ("Or do you not know…" v. 19), but this shift would also make sense if the third person statement were Paul's own thoughts.

4. *Proverbial Statements: Is there a potential slogan in the form of a generalization, like a proverbial statement (usually expressed in the present tense)?* Yes.

5. *Rhetorical Features: Are there rhetorical features, such as parallel structures, that might suggest an easy to memorize catchphrase?* No.

6. *Repetition: Are there expressions that are repeated at other points in the letter?* No.

7. *Diatribe: Are features of diatribe present or other rhetorical features that may suggest the presence of dialogue between the writer and others?* Yes. Here we need to pause and look at the passage as a whole.

There is significant evidence pointing to the use of diatribe in this section (6:12–20) of Paul's letter. First, we have the very likely presence of three Corinthian quotations in verses 12–13, indicating that Paul is presenting this portion of his letter in dialogic fashion. Second, Paul's question to the Corinthians in 6:15 introduces anticipated objections and false conclusions into his argument (a characteristic of diatribe); and this is met with an emphatic response from Paul: "Never!" (μὴ γένοιτο, *mē genoito*, another characteristic of diatribe). As we noted in chapter 3, diatribe typically makes use of a rhetorical dialogue between a writer and an imaginary or real interlocutor.[29] Notice also that Paul poses rhetorical questions three times to his interlocutors in his argument, each beginning with the phrase, "Do you not know" (vv. 15, 16, and 19).[30] Each of these questions is followed by Paul's rejection of the interlocutor's faulty thinking. The second question in 6:15 is followed by another rhetorical question based on the logical conclusion Paul infers from their flawed position: "Should I therefore take the members of Christ and make them members of a prostitute?" This rhetorical question is negated with the emphatic rejection, "Never!" (μὴ γένοιτο, *mē genoito*). Even without establishing the quotations in 6:12–13, the other

---

29. Burk, in his work on 6:12–20, makes a convincing argument for features of diatribe in this passage, with the quotations helping to establish a back and forth conversation between Paul and the Corinthians; "Discerning Corinthians Slogans," 99–121; see also Lambrecht, "Paul's Reasoning," 479–86.

30. Although we have noted in our study of diatribe in chapter 3 that dialogue was normally accomplished by the inclusion of an imaginary second-person conversation partner, Burk ("Discerning Corinthians Slogans," 105–21) has shown that by Paul's use of the second person plurals in 6:15, 16, and 19 ("do you all not know . . ."), he was signaling that the interlocutors were not imaginary in this case, but rather represented real factions in Corinth who were holding to concrete positions that Paul wished to correct.

features of diatribe in this passage would lead us to look for other ways that Paul directly engages the positions of his opponents. Murphy-O'Connor provides a helpful outline of the dialogue between Paul and the Corinthians in 6:12–20, which we have adapted using the NRSV and to reflect our analysis thus far:[31]

Interlocutor's Slogans	Paul's Rebuttal
(12) "All things are lawful for me" "All things are lawful for me"	but not all things are beneficial. but I will not be dominated by anything.
(13) "Food is meant for the stomach and the stomach for food"	and God will destroy both one and the other. The body is meant not for fornication but for the Lord, and the Lord for the body. (14) And God raised the Lord and will also raise us by his power. (15) DO YOU NOT KNOW that your bodies are members of Christ? Should I therefore take the members of Christ and make them members of a prostitute? Never! (16) DO YOU NOT KNOW that whoever is united to a prostitute becomes one body with her? For it is said, "The two shall be one flesh." (17) But anyone united to the Lord becomes one spirit with him. (18a) Shun fornication!
(18b) "Every sin that a person commits is outside the body"	but the fornicator sins against the body itself. (19) Or DO YOU NOT KNOW that your body is a temple of the Holy Spirit within you, which you have from God, and that you are not your own? (20) For you were bought with a price; therefore glorify God in your body.

---

31. Murphy-O'Connor, *1 Corinthians*, 50–51. See also Burk, "Discerning Corinthians Slogans," 113; Stowers, "A 'Debate' over Freedom," 68–69.

What we see, then, is substantial evidence for the use of diatribe in this passage as a whole. In 6:12–13, Paul begins his dialogue with the Corinthian factions by quoting slogans they have used to justify their immoral behavior. He responds to the flawed theology represented by each slogan in 6:12–14. In 6:15–17, the dialogue continues as Paul launches rhetorical questions at his interlocutors anticipating their objections and false conclusions. Paul then issues a simple corrective to their foolish thinking ("Shun fornication!" 6:18a) before quoting another possible misguided slogan in 6:18b. This final slogan of this passage he emphatically refutes by reminding them that their bodies are God's temple (6:19–20).[32] Thus we find Paul repeatedly quoting Corinthians as part of the diatribal argument he uses in this section of the letter.

8. *Contradictions: Are there statements that appear to contradict what the author says elsewhere in the same letter?* Yes. If Paul himself is making the assertion that "Every sin that a person commits is outside the body," he seems to be playing right into the Corinthians' hands. They were the ones who were arguing that sin does not matter because the body does not matter. So, "if it feels good, do it," whether that involves sex, food, or other indulgences. As we saw above, however, Paul sharply rebukes the Corinthians for their approach to food issues, whether it was food sacrificed to idols (1 Cor 8) or the Lord's Supper (1 Cor 11). It is difficult to conceive how Paul's teaching in those chapters could be reconciled with him asserting, "Every sin that a person commits is outside the body," especially when Christians are going to be bodily raised with Jesus and then transformed (e.g., 6:14; 15:51–56). Furthermore, as we stated above, Paul has just made it clear in 6:9–10 that certain behaviors are utterly incongruent with faith in Jesus Christ: "Fornicators, idolaters, adulterers, male prostitutes, sodomites, thieves, the greedy, drunkards, revilers, robbers— none of these will inherit the kingdom of God." And all of these were behaviors carried out with the body. Thus, "Every sin that a person commits is outside the body" would appear to be a contradiction if

---

32. Burk ("Discerning Corinthians Slogans," 112) states, "If this text does in fact comprise a special adaptation of the diatribe, then the phrase 'Every sin, whatever a person may do, is outside of the body' appears in precisely the place where we would expect Paul to introduce another objection. Since Paul has used slogans to form an objection in vv. 12 and 13, it is not unlikely that he would do so again in v. 18. Thus, the form of the diatribe in 6:12–20 suggests that v. 18 should also be understood as a Corinthian slogan."

it were stated by Paul himself, since if the sins listed in 6:9–10 were "outside the body," they should have no impact on whether a person committing them inherits the kingdom of God.

9. *Contrast: Does the writer present a sharp contrast or refutation to something he has just stated, which may have been a quotation? Or, does he make a statement and then provide commentary on that statement as if referring to something that has been expressed by others?* No. There is not a strong contrast, but there is an implicit contrast. Paul, once again, uses the conjunction δέ (*de*). Remember that this conjunction represents "the writer's choice to explicitly signal that what follows is a new development in the story or argument."[33] When that new development contrasts with what precedes, based on the context, the conjunction is naturally translated "but," as in the NRSV. More important, Paul appears to make a statement in the preceding clause ("Every sin that a person commits is outside the body") that he then comments on and refutes in the next clause ("but the fornicator [clearly] sins against his own body"[34]). This makes a contrast fairly obvious even without understanding how Greek conjunctions function.

10. *Common Issues: Are there expressions that may represent characteristic ways of thinking, based on the broad context of the letter, that the writer appears to be engaging with his audience?* Yes. We have seen in the near context that the Corinthians are proud of gross sexual sin among them (5:1–2, 6). And Paul has had to tell them "not to associate with anyone who bears the name of brother or sister who is sexually immoral or greedy, or is an idolater, reviler, drunkard, or robber. Do not even eat with such a one" (5:11). He then refers again to blatant sins that they may be deceived into thinking are acceptable (6:9–10). From our vantage point, it seems remarkable that Paul would have to confront any Christians about such absurd thinking. But when we come to verse 18, the statement there, read as the words of the Corinthians, helps us to understand *how* they were justifying such immoral behavior: "The so-called sins that some people are concerned about are not really sins at all because they are 'outside the body.'"

---

33. Runge, *Discourse Grammar*, 31; cf. Dooley and Levinsohn, *Analyzing Discourse*, 93.

34. Our translation.

11–12. Past Scholars and Common Sense: Is our assessment of a particular putative slogan consistent with the collective wisdom of Bible scholars and Bible translators? Does our assessment of a particular putative slogan pass the common sense test (i.e., does reading a particular text as a slogan or quotation make the best sense of the immediate context)? No. Past scholars do not support the view that Paul is quoting Corinthians here. Neither a majority of translations nor a majority of commentators see a quotation here. In fact, only two of the translations under consideration explicitly identify a quotation in 6:18:

> "Run from sexual immorality! 'Every sin a person can commit is outside the body.' On the contrary, the person who is sexually immoral sins against his own body." (HCSB)

> "Flee sexual immorality! 'Every sin a person commits is outside of the body' – but the immoral person sins against his own body." (NET)

Both of these versions include footnotes indicating some level of uncertainty regarding whether or not this verse includes a quotation. So, we find only very tepid support for a quotation among our English translations. What we do find, though, is something that should give us pause. Many of the English versions that do not identify a Corinthian slogan in 6:18b add the word "other" to their translation (e.g., NASV, NIV 1984, NIV 2011, ESV, and NJB): "All *other* sins a person commits . . ." (NIV). Without the use of "other," the next part of the verse (6:18c) seems to contradict the first part of the sentence (6:18b). With the use of "other" the statement is clearly marked as Paul's view, rather than the Corinthians'. The problem is that the word "other" has no basis in the Greek text. In fact, the Greek text is extremely emphatic and absolute in its reference to *all* sins: "Every sin whatsoever a man commits . . ."[35] Many of our English translations, then, have taken this absolute statement and weakened it by using the word "other" in an effort to remove the apparent contradiction between this statement and what Paul says next. The apparent contradiction, however, is completely removed (with no need to fudge on the translation), by simply recognizing that in 6:18b Paul is quoting the Corinthians.[36]

---

35. Our translation.

36. See also the helpful discussion in Burk, "Discerning Corinthians Slogans," 117–18.

What about modern scholars? Among the fifteen commentators we considered, Hays, Fitzmyer, Thiselton, Brookins/Longenecker, and Talbert all argue for a Corinthian slogan in 6:18. Keener agrees that a quotation is possible, while Blomberg, Barrett, Fee, Garland, and Witherington all reject the view that part of 6:18 is a quotation,[37] Conzelmann and Bruce do not address the issue at all, while Taylor and Ciampa/Rosner summarize the issues but do not land on a position. So, we find a very mixed bag among modern commentators, with fewer seeing a quotation here than those who do not. Indeed, Brookins has noted that only six of twenty commentaries published between 1965 and 2016 that he considered argued for a quotation here.[38] Our own analysis, on the other hand, using our twelve criteria, though not conclusive, points toward the view that Paul is quoting Corinthians once again in 6:18.

Paul's quotations of the three Corinthian slogans in 6:12–13 are, in fact, likely strengthened by the addition of yet another slogan in 6:18b that some Corinthians had embraced as a tool for justifying their sexual immorality. They had embraced the erroneous view that their bodily actions had nothing to do with sin. They had thus concluded that "All things are lawful for me" (6:12a, 12b). After all, "Food is meant for the stomach and the stomach for food" (6:13); and by application "Sex is meant for the body and the body for sex." While this seems absolutely absurd to us today, it makes sense for those who have come to believe that "Every sin that a person commits is outside the body" (6:18). If true sin takes place in a spiritual sphere, and that sphere has no connection to the physical sphere, then what one does with one's physical body is morally irrelevant.[39] Indeed, the Corinthians seem to have believed that since the body ceases to exist at death, it has no permanent value (see 6:14; and 1 Cor 15). To respond Paul showcases the incredibly high value God places on the body: he inhabits it by his Holy

---

37. So also Lambrecht, "Paul's Reasoning."

38. Brookins, *Corinthian Wisdom*, 92. Omanson ("Acknowledging Paul's Quotations," 207) also argues for a quotation here.

39. This is the thesis of Murphy-O'Connor ("Corinthian Slogans," 393). See also Smith's article, which supports Murphy-O'Connor's thesis; "Roots," 63–95. Thiselton (473) argues that Paul is citing a catchphrase used by his opponents here that he then counters. Note, however, the dissenting opinions of Lambrecht, "Paul's Reasoning," 479–86; Byrne, "Sinning against One's Own Body," 608–16; and Dodd, "Paul's Paradigmatic 'I'" and 1 Cor 6:12," 39–58.

Spirit (6:19)!⁴⁰ And he will go on in 1 Cor 15 to make it clear that the body does not cease to have value at death; it will be raised and transformed.

What about our common sense test? Commentators, to be frank, have struggled with 6:18. Ciampa and Rosner describe Paul's statement ("Every sin that a person commits is outside the body") as "one of the most puzzling in the letter."⁴¹ But when we acknowledge the likely presence of a Corinthian quotation in this otherwise difficult verse, the verse itself and the passage as a whole makes much better sense. Paul is continuing to engage the Corinthian argument. He once again rejects the false dichotomy some Corinthians have made between "spiritual" and "physical," and insists that what is done with the physical body is of extreme import, since God will raise up our physical bodies as he did Christ's (6:14).⁴² Not to mention the fact that the Holy Spirit actually inhabits our body *currently* (6:19).

Likelihood of a Quotation in 1 Cor 6:18: *Likely*. We might add that it is *more* likely than most English translations and scholars have recognized.

Theological Implications

So what are the implications when we recognize that Paul is interacting with Corinthian slogans in 6:12–20? How does this analysis impact how members of the Corinthian church would have understood Paul's words and how modern believers should understand and respond to this passage? Our analysis suggests that some Corinthian Christians were using libertine slogans to justify sexual immorality in their lives. They were boasting that "all things are permissible," even sexual depravity (5:1), since sexual appetites belong in the physical plane, which has nothing to do with the spiritual plane to which they now belonged.⁴³ If Paul's debate with the Corinthi-

---

40. If 6:18b is viewed as a Corinthian slogan, then it may provide further evidence that the slogan in 6:13a should end with "and God will destroy both one and the other," since the claims in both 6:13a and 6:18b offer false positions based on an inaccurate eschatological disconnect between physical earthly actions and eternal reality. Having said that, we would be left with one slogan (6:18) that meets the typical requirement for a "slogan" (it is pithy), and one that reads more like a long statement (6:13).

41. Ciampa and Rosner, 263.

42. As Murphy O'Connor notes, "If the body is to be the object of a divine action, if it is to benefit by a display of divine power, it cannot be unimportant" ("Corinthian Slogans," 395).

43. The Corinthians who espoused this slogan quite possibly argued that Paul was

ans were occurring today, he might have quoted them saying something like, "We're all about grace here!" Or, "We're a grace-based church, not a rules-based church!" Or, "God has already forgiven us for whatever sins we commit!" Or, "When God looks at you, he sees Jesus regardless of your behavior!" Paul, however, refutes this faulty theological perspective by arguing that their immoral desires are actually trapping them in bondage to sin, the very thing from which Christ had died to free them. Blomberg rightly suggests that "12b reflects a Greek word play that could be approximated in English by translating, 'All things are in my power, but I shall not be overpowered by anything.'"[44] The gospel that Paul proclaimed was a gospel of freedom from sin, not a gospel that brought freedom *to* sin.

As Paul's argument makes clear, however, his opponents in Corinth had a well-constructed rationale for their position. So, he must address their other arguments for their libertine position, which again are expressed as slogans. To seek to further justify their contention that anything goes ("All things are lawful for me") they made use of another popular slogan: "food for the stomach and the stomach for food" (our translation). This was almost certainly a euphemistic[45] way of saying, "Sex for the body and the body for sex," or "The sexual organs are for sex and sex is for the sexual organs."[46] Some among the Corinthians appear to have essentially believed

---

the one they got the idea from in the first place. We see this very problem emerging in the church in Rome among Paul's opponents, who claimed that his law-free gospel promoted sin (e.g., Rom 3:8; 6:1, 15). Here, the difference would be that while some in Rome rejected Paul's gospel because they wrongly viewed it as promoting sin, some of the Corinthians thought they were taking Paul's gospel to its logical conclusion by embracing both it and the anything-goes lifestyle they wrongly thought it promoted.

44. Blomberg, 126.

45. Euphemism involves speaking about something that is unpleasant or taboo in an indirect way using a more agreeable expression. Thus, rather than saying, "My dad died," we say, "My dad passed away."

46. Blomberg notes (126) that although the slogan, "Food for the stomach and the stomach for food," could reflect a reference to their new freedom from the Jewish dietary laws, "apart from these contexts the slogans virtually invite people to sin, as the Corinthians apparently were doing. Hence Paul explains that Christians still must submit to moral principles ... because many things simply are not beneficial and not truly liberating." Those who see a longer quote here maintain that the Corinthians went on to argue that we all know that "God will destroy both one" (the stomach) "and the other" (food), once this temporal age passes away. In other words, since the body will ultimately be destroyed, it stands to reason that the body has no moral or spiritual relevance. Thus, the Corinthian group is attempting to create "a sense of distance between deeds done in the physical body ... and the supposedly 'spiritual' level of life" (Thiselton, 462).

that as long as a believer's inner life was healthy, what the believer did outwardly, or with their body, was of no consequence (6:18b).

While we do not find this exact type of thinking commonly appearing in churches today, we do find similar ways of thinking. For example, many professing Christians—whether they would admit it or not—believe that since they are bound for heaven, "What difference does it ultimately make how we live now?" After all, "We all sin thousands of times every day anyway? What's an extra sin or two?" "God is going to forgive us anyway." You see, we too have our own slogans that we use to justify our sin, despite the fact that God clearly says in Scripture, "as he who called you is holy, be holy yourselves in all your conduct; for it is written, 'You shall be holy, for I am holy'" (1 Pet 1:15–16). Elsewhere, God tells us, "But fornication and impurity of any kind, or greed, must not even be mentioned among you, as is proper among saints" (Eph 5:3), but we use popular ways of thinking—that even sound spiritual—to justify ignoring these sky-high standards that God calls us to. We, like the Corinthians, need to have our slogans dismantled and identified as the flawed thinking they are.

How does Paul respond to the Corinthians' thinking? He makes it clear that the believer's current physical existence is presently united with God by the indwelling presence of the Holy Spirit (6:19). Thus, it is ridiculous to believe that we have license to indulge our bodies with sin while we await the eschaton, since as surely as Christ was raised by the power of God, so the children of God will be bodily raised by this same power. Our "bodies are members of Christ" right now (6:15)! Thus, when we participate in immoral acts, we are involving *Christ's members* in sinful activities.[47] Paul, therefore, asks with utter dismay, "Should I therefore take the members of Christ and make them members of a prostitute? Never!" (6:15).

Finally, Paul seeks to refute the apparent Corinthian view that "Every sin that a person commits is outside of the body" (6:18). This flawed theological position builds on their inaccurate conviction that so-called sexual sins are really of no eternal importance since the body is of no eternal consequence.[48] Sin, in the Corinthian view, simply has no impact on the body or the person committing the sin. Sin comes from the heart; what one does

---

47. See the similar argument in Rom 6.

48. This view did not mean that the party denied the existence of sin, but that they viewed sin as taking place on a sphere different than the physical sphere (i.e., the heart, mind, motives, and intentions); see Murphy-O'Connor, *1 Corinthians*, 51. See also Smith ("Roots," 76–84), who suggests that this popular libertinism in Paul's day may have had its origins in Stoic and other later Hellenistic-Roman thought including Gnosticism.

with his or her body is, therefore, irrelevant. Sexual intercourse, then, is viewed simply as a natural physical desire to be satisfied in the same manner that physical hunger and physical thirst should be satisfied. It is a bodily function that has no relationship to sin or morality.

Paul, of course, will not leave such nonsense unrefuted. He has already made it clear that while the present body will be "destroyed" (6:13), its destruction will come through resurrection. And there will be significant continuity between the physical body and the coming spiritual body, which Paul will later make clear through the extended metaphor of a seed growing into something that looks very different than the seed and yet *comes from* the seed (15:35–38). In this context, Paul first emphasizes the need to "Shun fornication!" Then, acknowledging the Corinthian slogan, he proceeds to make it crystal clear that the person who chooses to use his or her body for sexual sin actually sins against their body. Worse than that, Paul makes clear, that person also sins against the Lord. The body does not become insignificant for those who become followers of Jesus. Instead, its significance is infinitely increased, since the body of a believer is the temple that the Holy Spirit now inhabits (6:19). Furthermore, just as a person generally lives in a house they own, so the Holy Spirit's residence in the body of the believer indicates that God now owns those he has redeemed. And those whom God owns must live for God's glory, not for their own desires (6:20).

7

The Corinthians and Sexuality

Asceticism

What is remarkable in 1 Corinthians is that we appear to find two dramatically different approaches to sexuality operating within the same congregation, or at least within congregations in the same city. While some believed that what Christians did with their bodies was irrelevant because they were now spiritual people (thus sexual promiscuity was acceptable to them), others believed that as spiritual people they had no need for sexual relations, even within marriage (asceticism). Thus, although Paul continues to respond to Corinthian perspectives on sexual relationships in 1 Cor 7, there is a shift to sexual relationships within marriage, a shift from addressing libertine attitudes to addressing ascetic attitudes, and a shift from addressing inappropriate sexual activity to addressing appropriate sexual activity. These shifts suggest that Paul is now responding to a different faction among the Corinthians.

In 1 Cor 6, Paul dealt with the issue of inappropriate sexual relationships outside of marriage and corrected a faction that believed that illicit sexual relationships outside of marriage were irrelevant to one's relationship with God. Their faulty beliefs were expressed in slogans. Now, beginning in 7:1, Paul moves to the issue of sexual relationships within marriage in an effort to correct a group among the Corinthians who were apparently advocating celibacy for those who were married.[1] There seems to have been no

---

1. Fee (273n25) notes that the suggestion that 7:1 contains a Corinthian slogan goes as far back as the time of Origen (ca. 200 CE). See also Fee's convincing argument in

end to the nonsense that was being dreamed up in the church at Corinth! This time, though, Paul does not engage Corinthian slogans. Instead, he responds to a question about sex within marriage that came to him by way of a letter sent to him from Corinth: "it is reasonable to regard the περὶ δέ (*peri de*) ["now concerning"] formula as introducing a direct quotation or paraphrase from the Corinthians' letter that serves as a subject heading for the section: sexual asceticism and marriage."[2]

1 Corinthians 7:1–6

> "Now concerning the matters about which you wrote: 'It is well for a man not to touch a woman.' 2 But because of cases of sexual immorality, each man should have his own wife and each woman her own husband. 3 The husband should give to his wife her conjugal rights, and likewise the wife to her husband. 4 For the wife does not have authority over her own body, but the husband does; likewise the husband does not have authority over his own body, but the wife does. 5 Do not deprive one another except perhaps by agreement for a set time, to devote yourselves to prayer, and then come together again, so that Satan may not tempt you because of your lack of self-control. 6 This I say by way of concession, not of command."

Although we would not realize it by simply reading the NRSV, given its use of quotation marks in 7:1, it is not immediately clear whether Paul is citing the Corinthians' position or his own. The verse could also be translated, "Now concerning the matters about which you wrote. It is well for a man not to touch a woman." In this case, "It is well for a man not to touch a woman" would be the first part of *Paul's* argument. And such a reading would provide a strong basis for celibacy. So, what did Paul intend to communicate here? Let's consider how our twelve steps can help us answer that question.

"1 Corinthians in the NIV," 307–14; cf. Garland, 251, 254–55. For a counter view, see Caragounis, "'Fornication' and 'Concession'?," 543–59; cf. Fitzmyer, 274, 278.

2. Garland, 249. See our previous discussion on the issues surrounding Paul's use of περὶ δέ (*peri de*) in chapter 2 above.

Twelve Steps for Identifying Quotations: 1 Cor 7:1

1. *Context: Does the context lead us to expect a quotation?* Yes. Paul's use of "now concerning" along with "the matters about which you wrote" make a subsequent quote very natural.

2. *Quotative Frame: Is there a "quotative frame" in the near context?* Yes. The phrase, "you wrote," may be viewed as a (weaker) quotative frame.

3. *Shift in Person: Is there a shift in grammatical "person"?* Yes. There is a shift from second person in "you wrote" to third person in the clause that follows.

4. *Proverbial Statements: Is there a potential slogan in the form of a generalization, like a proverbial statement (usually expressed in the present tense)?* Yes.

5. *Rhetorical Features: Are there rhetorical features, such as parallel structures, that might suggest an easy to memorize catchphrase?* No.

6. *Repetition: Are there expressions that are repeated at other points in the letter?* No.

7. *Diatribe: Are features of diatribe present or other rhetorical features that may suggest the presence of dialogue between the writer and others?* Yes. The reference to the matters about which the Corinthians wrote clearly indicates that Paul is about to dialogue with one or more of their positions.

8. *Contradictions: Are there statements that appear to contradict what the author says elsewhere in the same letter?* Yes. The possible quote ("it is good for a man not to touch a woman") appears to contradict the high value Paul places on sexual relations within marriage in the immediate context (7:3–5).

9. *Contrast: Does the writer present a sharp contrast or refutation to something he has just stated, which may have been a quotation? Or, does he make a statement and then provide commentary on that statement as if referring to something that has been expressed by others?* Yes. He offers commentary in what follows as if referring to something that has been expressed by others. He introduces this commentary with the conjunction δέ (*de*), which signals that he is presenting the

next development in his argument.³ The content of the statement also sharply contrasts with the apparent quotation.

10. *Common Issues: Are there expressions that may represent characteristic ways of thinking, based on the broad context of the letter, that the writer appears to be engaging with his audience?* Yes. Initially, one is tempted to say, "No," since the Corinthians seem to have taken an "anything goes" approach to sexuality (see 1 Cor 5–6). But Paul is addressing a new problem in this passage, a problem that the Corinthians themselves had raised with him in *their* letter. Many had boasted about letting grace abound when a man was shacking up with his step-mother; but there were *others* who had taken the position that sex should be avoided even within marriage. It is to that apparently minority position that Paul responds here. What the two positions have in common is a warped sense of how the physical realm is related to the spiritual realm.

11–12. *Past Scholars and Common Sense: Is our assessment of a particular putative slogan consistent with the collective wisdom of Bible scholars and Bible translators? Does our assessment of a particular putative slogan pass the common sense test (i.e., does reading a particular text as a slogan or quotation make the best sense of the immediate context)?*

How have English translations, besides the NRSV, handled this passage? There are actually two related issues that need to be considered. First, does the translation explicitly identify the second half of 7:1 as the Corinthians' position through the use of quotations marks? Second, how is the word ἅπτεσθαι (*haptesthai*) translated? Since the second question somewhat determines how the various translations deal with the first question, we will consider it first.

The Greek word ἅπτεσθαι (*haptesthai*) generally simply means "to touch" (see, e.g., Louw and Nida 24.73); and this is the way most modern English versions translate it here (NRSV, NASB, NKJV, NJB, MEV). Other versions, however, translate the phrase "touch a woman" "have sexual relations" (ESV; NET, NIV 2011) or "have relations with" (HCSB). This is consistent with the fact that the verb may be used as part of a phrase to convey a variety of ideas where "touching" is involved. Thus, some writers

---

3. Thiselton (501) wrongly suggests that after the quotation, "the adversative particle δέ [*de*] needs to be rendered with due force, such as On the contrary," to show Paul's rejection of the notion beginning in 7:2. Thiselton's argument would have required Paul to use the conjunction ἀλλά (*alla*) rather than δέ (*de*).

contemporaneous with the New Testament used this same verb in the phrase, "to touch food," in order to communicate "to eat."[4] The NIV (1984), on the other hand, has almost certainly missed the point by translating the whole phrase (formally, "to touch a woman") as "to marry."[5] Not only is this contextually implausible—putting a reference to marriage into Paul's mouth at this point makes a mess of his argument—but it also fails to recognize the use of a common expression for sexual relations here.[6] The issue Paul is addressing concerns the appropriateness of sexual relations within marriage, with the expression, "to touch a woman," simply being a euphemism for sexual intercourse.[7] This reading fits with Paul's following words directing that each man "have his own wife" (7:2), likely another euphemism for sexual intercourse with one's wife. Why is it critical that a husband engage in sexual relations with his wife? It is critical "because of the temptation to sexual immorality" (7:2).

That brings us back to our first issue: Is verse 7:1b Paul's opinion or is he quoting the Corinthians? Once we rule out the problematic translation "to marry" in 7:1b as untenable—given both the context and the use of the Greek expression elsewhere—it becomes very likely that Paul is quoting the Corinthians in 7:1b. After all, Paul goes on to emphasize in the immediate context the importance of spouses not depriving one another of sexual relations (7:5). Beyond the context, however, we also have the clear reference to an issue that the Corinthians had raised in their letter, to which Paul is now going to respond: "Now concerning the matters about which you wrote" (7:1a). If 7:1b were read as Paul's immediate response to some general issue contained in the letter from Corinth, he would be providing no context to indicate what that matter was. On the other hand, if we read 7:1b as Paul quoting the Corinthians' letter, all that follows makes perfect sense as Paul's response.

---

4. See the entry for ἅπτω (*haptō*) in BDAG, 126.3.

5. This same mistranslation is found in the Good News Bible and the Spanish and French Common Language versions; Omanson, "Acknowledging Paul's Quotations," 207. The Spanish and French translations likely followed the GNB here.

6. The NIV translators likely read the context of 7:8–9 back into 7:1, unfortunately ignoring the verses that immediately follow 7:1; see Omanson, "Acknowledging Paul's Quotations," 207.

7. Fee (275) notes that of the nine times the expression, "to touch a woman," is found in ancient Greek literature, each time it refers to sexual intercourse. Hays (113) adds that in Greek literature, "this expression is never used to mean 'to marry,' as the NIV [1984] translates it."

Now let us consider how the various translations treat the potential quotation. Six of the translations put 7:1b in quotation marks, indicating that the translators viewed this clause as the position of some in Corinth, although the translations differ in wording (NRSV, NIV 2011, NET, ESV, MEV, HCSB). These translations leave readers to naturally assume that Paul then corrects the faulty Corinthian thinking expressed in 7:1b in what follows. The NJB, on the other hand, does not use quotation marks, but does imply that a quotation is in view: "Now concerning the *questions* about which you wrote." With this approach to 7:1a the translators were then free not to use quotes in 7:1b, since they clearly indicate that Paul is affirming the Corinthian position: "Yes, it is good for a man not to touch a woman." This makes 7:1b consistent with Paul's teaching in 7:8–9, while still identifying it as originating from the Corinthians' letter and also allowing Paul to nuance this view in what follows: "*yet* to avoid immorality every man should have his own wife and every woman her own husband" (7:2; NJB). The weakness of the NJB translation, however, is that the context (Paul insisting on marital rights) makes it clear that Paul could never affirm the appropriateness of the Corinthians' position. In what follows, he does not nuance a shared position; he *refutes* a position that he rejects outright.

The three remaining translations under review (NIV 1984, NKJV, NASB) translate 7:1b without quotations marks, leaving readers likely to infer that Paul is stating his own opinion. As can be seen from our discussion above, these translations easily lead readers to misread Paul's argument in this portion of the letter.

The commentaries we considered are ultimately consistent in maintaining that Paul is either quoting a specific Corinthian slogan or a particular line from the Corinthians' letter in 7:1b.[8] Conzelmann argues that 7:1 points to direct questions that were sent to Paul from Corinth that expected answers from the apostle.[9] Thus, beginning in 7:2, Paul is giving a direct answer to the first question posed by the Corinthians, with other questions

---

8. Two commentators (Barrett and Fitzmyer) seem hesitant to wholly commit to the prospect that Paul is not citing his own position here, but each finally agrees that the apostle is likely stating a quotation from the Corinthian letter. Fitzmyer (278; cf. Barrett, 154) notes that "the statement may reflect a debate among Christians of Corinth; if it does, it might have been a slogan in use among them . . . In this instance, however, it is far from certain that it is a slogan, because it might also be a Pauline answer to a question posed in the letter that he has received."

9. Conzelmann (115) believes that the Corinthians were confused by Paul's previous letter (see 5:9) concerning sexual immorality, and essentially the question being asked of Paul is, "Is sexual intercourse allowed (at all)?"

being found in 7:25; 8:1; 12:1; and 16:1, 12.[10] This is certainly possible, but it does not significantly impact our analysis.

What about our common sense test? Does reading the text with a quotation make the best sense of the passage? Paul goes on to point out that marriage can distract one from working for God's kingdom (7:32–35); not to mention that marriage also brings "worldly troubles" (7:28). This may seem to imply that he is making a statement about the inferiority of marriage here. As we consider the overall context, however, it becomes clear that Paul is not promoting celibacy within marriage. And when we combine the evidence from the context with the fact that Paul uses the περὶ δέ (*peri de*, "now concerning") formula to indicate that he is about to interact with an explicit position from the Corinthians, it is virtually certain that that position is introduced in the clause that the NRSV marks as a quotation.

Once we acknowledge that Paul is quoting a Corinthian slogan in 7:1b, the remainder of this passage makes perfect sense. Paul indicates his disagreement with the Corinthian slogan and proceeds to refute their flawed view in 7:2–5. The irony, of course, is that in 1 Cor 6 Paul argues that participating in sex outside of marriage is wrong, while in 1 Cor 7 he argues that abstaining from sex within marriage is wrong. His need to address both of these issues highlights the tendency for extreme views within the Corinthian church. On the issue of sex, we find the "anything goes" view coexisting with the "no sex allowed in any circumstances" view within the same church.[11] The sexual perversion that permeated Corinthian society had led some within the church to justify following the world around them, while it had thoroughly confused others to the point that they were throwing the baby out with the bathwater and rejecting sexual relations altogether, even within marriage. That this was problematic should have been obvious to the Corinthians in view, since the stance that "it is good for a man not to touch a woman" utterly contradicted the divine ordinance found in Gen 2:18: "it is *not good* for the man to be alone."[12]

Likelihood of a Quotation in 7:1: *Very Likely*

---

10. Ibid.

11. Garland (243) notes that Paul's statement in 7:28 arguing that those who marry do not commit sin suggests that others in Corinth must have rejected the flawed view that argued for absolute abstinence.

12. Thiselton, 501.

A CLOSER LOOK

Sexual Attitudes in Corinth

Even a casual reader of 1 Corinthians will notice the substantial emphasis that is placed on the topic of sexual relationships in this letter. As we noted above, the church in Corinth often mirrored the openness to illicit sexual activity that was found in the city of Corinth. Corinth was a hotbed of sexual opportunities, in part, no doubt, to service the countless sailors that arrived at the city's two ports, but more broadly evidenced by the abundance of pagan temples and religious rituals that clearly had sexual connotations.

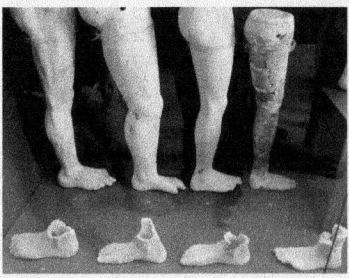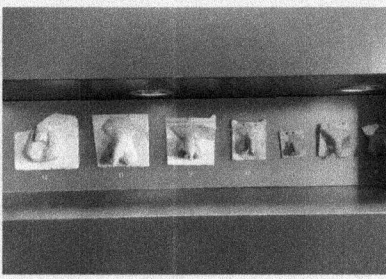

Figures 8 and 9: Pictures of clay body parts that were part of the Asclepius Cult (god of healing). People would make a representation of the body part they were seeking to be healed. The many examples of male genitalia points to the large number of people at Corinth who were seeking healing from sexually transmitted diseases during this time period.

There is some dispute regarding Corinth's reputation in the first century. Some scholars maintain that although Greek Corinth had an overblown reputation for sexual license, Roman Corinth (during Paul's day) was not necessarily the same.[13] Achtemeier, Green, and Thompson, on the other hand, cite evidence from Dio Chrysostom writing in the first century: "The orator Dio Chrysostom remarked that large numbers of people gathered at Corinth because of the good harbors and the 'female companions,' (*Discourse* 8.5) and noted that Corinth was known for its elegant and elaborate women, leading to the proverb 'Not every man can afford the trip to Corinth' (*Discourse* 20.7). The name of Corinth became the base for words coined to refer to various forms of sexual behavior."[14] Whether or not first-century Corinth was as sexually permissive as the old city, the fact that it was "a rough, relatively new boomtown adjacent to two seaports,"[15] and a main thoroughfare between Rome and the East likely made modern comparisons to Las Vegas appropriate at a certain level. It is likely appropriate to say that Corinth was a city that was known as a place where you could "have a good time." After all, "What happens in Corinth stays in Corinth!" Unlike Las Vegas, however, much of the debauchery that was prevalent in Corinth was linked to the religions that were active there and elsewhere in the Roman Empire.

---

13. Carson and Moo, *An Introduction to the New Testament*, 420.

14. Achtemeier, Green, and Thompson, *Introducing the New Testament*, 328–29.

15. Brown, *An Introduction to the New Testament*, 513.

Theological Implications

How does recognizing the presence of a Corinthian quotation in this passage impact how Christians today should respond to this portion of the New Testament? Over the centuries, some faith traditions have held up asceticism (believing that forms of rigorous self-denial contribute to one's spirituality) as the ideal for followers of Jesus Christ. There appears to have been a hint of this approach to life within the church at Corinth, at least with regard to sex. As Bruce notes,

> The transition from chapter 6 to chapter 7 illustrates the necessity Paul was under of waging a campaign on two fronts. In chapter 6 he dealt with the libertines who argued that everything was permissible... in chapter 7 he deals with ascetics who, partly perhaps in reaction against the libertines, argued that sexual relations of every kind were to be deprecated, that Christians who were married should henceforth live as though they were unmarried, and those who were unmarried should remain so, even if they were already engaged to be married.[16]

Paul's quotations of the Corinthian positions certainly support Bruce's analysis. And the mutually incompatible views that he refutes make it clear that Paul was dealing with factions within the church at Corinth, which in both cases had embraced unbiblical views of sexuality.[17] To these factions Paul makes it clear that just as sex outside of marriage is a problem for one whose body is now the temple of the Holy Spirit (6:12–20), so also lack of sex within marriage is a problem for followers of Jesus (7:1b–7), and is, in fact, dangerous.[18]

The assertion of some Corinthians that one should practice celibacy even within marriage is consistent with other ascetic positions Paul addressed elsewhere (cf. Col 2:21–22; 1 Tim 4:3).[19] Some scholars posit that this ascetic impulse likely flowed out of an over-realized eschatology—the view that they had already "arrived" and fully entered into the spiritual benefits of the age to come.[20] We see elsewhere in 1 Corinthians that some

---

16. Bruce, 66.

17. Keener (63), however, suggests that it is possible that the same group who justified sexual license in 1 Cor 6 could be opposing marriage in 1 Cor 7.

18. Ibid., 62.

19. For examples of higher esteem being given to celibacy in Greek philosophy, see Conzelmann, 115.

20. See Thiselton, "Realized Eschatology," 510–26; Talbert, 38; cf. Garland, 264–65; Cartlidge, "1 Corinthians 7," 227–30.

within the church seem to have believed that they spoke in the tongues of angels (13:1), some denied the resurrection (15:12, 19), and some seemed to think they were already enjoying the fullness of life in Christ (4:8). In our culture, we sometimes speak of someone being "so heavenly minded that they're no earthly good." In most cases, the more heavenly minded someone is—seeking first God's kingdom and His righteousness; denying themselves, taking up their cross, and following Jesus—the more earthly good they will be. But that is not always true. In the case of the Corinthians, they had become so "spiritual" *in their own eyes* that they were denying at least one of the natural features of their physical existence that had been created by God and declared good: sex within marriage. This ascetic impulse was almost certainly used, as was the gift of tongues in Corinth, as a means of self-promotion: "Look how spiritual I am! I not only speak in tongues all the time, I have no need for making love to my wife!"[21]

Paul, of course, utterly rejects this view.[22] Although Paul does not find marriage personally appealing, he is far from forbidding others to marry, and in the verses that follow his quotation of the Corinthians (7:1b), he sets forth the reasons why the Corinthian position is so problematic. Paul's response is presented in a chiastic structure (an A B C C' B' A' pattern):

A. Temptation (v. 2)
   B. Marital sex is encouraged (v. 3)
      C. Dependence of woman on man (4a)
      C'. Dependence of man on woman (4b)
   B'. Marital sex is encouraged (v. 5a)
A'. Temptation (v. 5b)[23]

---

21. Although we cannot be sure of the Corinthians' rationale for abstinence within marriage, if some of them believed that they were not only called to speak the language of angels (1 Cor 13:1) but also to live like the angels, perhaps they had misappropriating Jesus' words about living in heaven like the angels (unmarried; see Matt 22:30; Mark 12:25; Luke 20:34–35) and concluded that sexual activity with their spouses should be discontinued. See Talbert, 37–38.

22. Hays (117) adds that in light of a correct reading of this text, "we can see how disastrously misinterpreted this passage has been by much of the Christian tradition. The time-honored reading of this text sees Paul as grudgingly permitting marriage itself as a distasteful concession to the lusts of the flesh. In fact, however, it is some of the Corinthians who are seeking to renounce marriage and sexual intercourse, and it is Paul who insists in a robustly realistic way that sexual relations within marriage are normal and necessary."

23. For a variation of this pattern, see Garland, 246; Talbert, 38.

A. Temptation (v. 2): Paul begins by making it clear that to avoid the temptations associated with the sexual immorality described in 6:12–21, each man must "have" his own wife and each wife must "have" her own husband. As was noted above, this is a euphemism for sexual intercourse. Thus, Paul is asserting that healthy, regular sexual relations within marriage are a necessary safeguard against sexual immorality.

B. Marital sex is encouraged (v. 3): In verse 3, Paul introduces the notion of rights into the argument. Although various conjugal rights and obligations were associated with marriage in the ancient world, as is evident in the extant marriage contracts from the period, here Paul is clearly referring to sexual intercourse, affirming the goodness of sexual intercourse within the context of marriage. More than that, he is portraying sexual relations as the responsibility of both the husband and the wife. Notably, there is no preferential treatment for males; both men and women have recognized conjugal rights that must be honored.

C. Dependence of woman on man (v. 4a); C'. Dependence of man on woman (v. 4b): Again in verse 4 we see how Scripture affords higher honor to females than was often common in the ancient world. Although it was well established in ancient societies that the husband had authority over the wife's body, and could therefore expect her to accommodate his sexual needs, it was not particularly common to acknowledge that the wife had the same authority over her husband's body. When it came to sexual rights within marriage, Paul made it clear that the husband and the wife were on equal footing.[24] This should not be surprising since Paul is careful to demonstrate the equal status of males and females elsewhere and to issue commands calling both to deny themselves and put their spouse above themselves (see, e.g., 1 Cor 11:11–12; Gal 3:28; Eph 5:22–33; Col 3:18–19). Keener suggests that the sexual rights Paul describes here for both husband and wife over the other's body naturally flow out of the notion of married couples being "one flesh" (6:16).[25]

B'. Marital sex is encouraged (v. 5a): In verse 5, Paul once again not only encourages sexual relations between husband and wife, but also stipulates that sex should be enjoyed *often* by married couples. This drives home the point that Paul, writing under the inspiration of the Holy Spirit,

---

24. Discussions of gender relations arising in 1 Cor 11 and 14 often neglect to recognize what Paul says here.

25. Keener, 62. In 6:16, of course, Paul's concern is with those who would enter into a one flesh relationship with a prostitute.

does not approve of sexual abstinence within marriage. Indeed, such abstinence should only occur (1) for spiritual reasons, such as devoting oneself to prayer; (2) when it can be limited to a set period of time (presumably short); and (3) by mutual consent. The last point once again highlights the equal rights that Scripture gives to husbands and wives in regard to sex. If a husband unilaterally decides that as the head of the household he is going to abstain from sex with his wife for thirty days, he is sinning against God and likely violating Scripture on two counts (it is a long period of time and he did not obtain his wife's consent). We might add, in today's context, that if a husband refuses to give his wife her conjugal rights because he has satisfied his sexual needs through the use of pornography, he is sinning against both his wife and God. His body does not belong to himself only; it also belongs to his wife.

A'. Temptation (v. 5b): To drive home the command to avoid significant periods of abstinence Paul provides a reason. Failing to satisfy one's sexual needs with one's spouse provides Satan with an opportunity to tempt followers of Jesus. If they are not able to exercise self-control, they may easily succumb to temptation to satisfy their sexual needs in another way. In the ancient world, the common practice would be through prostitution or an adulterous relationship. In the modern world, the temptation to find a prostitute has largely been replaced with the far simpler and less conspicuous method of indulging in internet pornography or other types of electronic illicit behaviors.

Paul, though, is not done with correcting the warped Corinthian view that sexual relations should be avoided within marriage. In 7:6, he writes, "This I say by way of concession, not of command." Here, he is not saying that regular sex within marriage is a concession; nor is he suggesting that marriage itself is a concession. Instead, it is abstinence from sex within marriage for a limited time period in order to devote oneself to prayer that is the concession.[26] Paul is not absolutely opposed to abstinence within the marriage relationship, but he wants to be careful to ensure that the Corinthians not interpret what he has just said as a command to abstain from sexual relations with one's spouse for periods of devotion to prayer. Paul does not want to put any Christian in harm's way, and he recognizes that

---

26. For examples from the Old Testament, ancient Jewish literature, and later rabbinic literature where temporary abstinence from sexual relations within marriage is found, see Conzelmann, 117; Garland, 261; Talbert, 38–39.

the temptation that often comes with such abstinence is not something to be taken lightly or something that everyone can handle.[27]

Finally, in the verse that follows this sub-section (7:7), Paul writes: "I wish that all were as I myself am. But each has a particular gift from God, one having one kind and another a different kind."[28] Paul often uses himself as a model for other believers to imitate (cf. 4:16; 11:1). What is his point here? As a single Christian man, Paul would have led a celibate life. This is often viewed as a form of self-denial or suffering, and throughout church history it has been held in high esteem by some believers as being a superior and more spiritual state than marriage. Does Paul, though, advocate celibacy over marriage in this passage? If we ended our investigation with 7:7a, we could plausibly argue this view; but Paul does not end there. Instead, he goes on to say that "each has a particular gift from God, one having one kind and another a different kind" (7:7b). Notice that Paul implies that both marriage and celibacy are "gifts from God." They are different, but they are both *gifts*. To those with the gift of living unmarried, Spirit-empowered self-control extends to being capable of living normally without sexual relations. Even though Paul has a preference for his own gift, he does not diminish the state of marriage.

Paul will acknowledge later in the chapter that marriage will create distractions for followers of Christ, because they will be torn between pleasing their spouse and being totally devoted to God (7:25–40); but Paul is very aware that not everyone is called/gifted to live a single and celibate

---

27. In the traditional reading of this passage, which has Paul himself making the statement, "It is well for a man not to touch a woman," the concession in verse 6 may refer to the "but because" in verse 2 or to all of verses 2–5. In this case, Paul's message would be that it is a concession to get married and only allowable because people are weak and cannot abstain from sexual immorality. Marriage, then, would be a way to avoid immorality. This view holds marriage and sex in very low esteem and is not in agreement with the plan of God from creation (Gen 2:18).

28. When Paul writes, "I wish all men to be as I am," Talbert (39) believes that this is actually a slogan coming from the same Corinthian faction we find in 7:1, who are here attempting to use a common Pauline slogan for their own position of sexual celibacy. He notes that although the words are obviously Paul's as he uses them elsewhere (cf. 1 Cor 4:6; 11:1; Gal 4:12), in this context they do not reflect Paul's position, since Paul does not wish all men to be unmarried. The faction is attempting to say that "since Paul wants us to imitate him, we should live a single life as Paul does." Yet, we see that Paul disagrees with their use of his slogan, unless one has been called by God to do so (see 7:7–24). Ultimately, we believe the passage makes more sense with these words taken as Paul's own opinion. He is stating what he views as an ideal, but recognizes that God has different plans for different people.

life. So, in 7:7, after making his preference clear—that other believers would stay single as he is—he is quick to acknowledge that God does not intend singleness for everyone. And some (or most) will, therefore, do well to marry, lest they "burn with passion" (7:9).

8

The Corinthians and Community

Appeals to Advantage

In his rhetoric in 1 Corinthians, Paul regularly utilizes what is known as "the appeal to advantage." This technique was commonly found in Greco-Roman deliberative rhetoric, where an author or orator attempted to convince an audience that it was in their best interest to follow a proposed course of action.[1] Paul's first use of the appeal to advantage was found in 6:12, where he quotes the Corinthian position ("all things are lawful to me"), and then qualifies the slogan with his own proposition ("but not everything is advantageous"). In that case, Paul's refutation of the Corinthian error followed the rationale that despite what a person *can* do, one must make choices that impact the greater good of the individual. And for a believer, the greater good should be viewed in light of a correct understanding of God's intention for the body in regard to sin (6:12b, 13b) and the central purpose of those redeemed by God: to glorify him with their bodies (6:19–20).

In 1 Cor 8–10, Paul uses the appeal to advantage once more, but this time he redefines where the best interests of the Corinthians are to be found. Once again, Paul's argument will flow out of the foundational truth he expressed in 6:19: "you are not your own." The pursuit of personal happiness is paramount when one is the master of one's own destiny; but for those

---

1. Aristotle notes that the deliberative orator must argue for the greater good or greater expediency of one proposed course of action over another (*Rhet.* 1.7.1). For further examples of the appeal to advantage in ancient literature, see Mitchell, *Paul and the Rhetoric of Reconciliation*, 25–39.

who belong to Another, everything changes. In these three chapters, Paul makes it clear that personal decisions can no longer be based on what is in one's own best interests, because followers of Jesus are now part of the Body of Christ. They are corporately[2] "God's temple," and decisions must therefore prioritize what is best for the entire community. When Paul repeats the Corinthians' slogan in 10:23 ("all things are lawful"), he refutes it with an appeal to the advantage of the community in 10:24 ("do not seek your own advantage, but that of the other"). Paul will then use himself as a model of decision-making based on community advantage in 10:33 ("not seeking *my own* advantage, but that of the many"). This rhetorical shift echoes the heart of the entire argument found in chapters 8–12 (and in reality the whole of the letter). "Paul wisely redefines the Corinthians' assumed goal from self-interest to community interest in order to persuade them to work for the common good."[3] To accomplish this goal, he once again appears to quote some of the Corinthians (potential quotations in italics below).

1 Corinthians 8:1–13

> "Now concerning food sacrificed to idols: we know that '*all of us possess knowledge.*' Knowledge puffs up, but love builds up. 2 Anyone who claims to know something does not yet have the necessary knowledge; 3 but anyone who loves God is known by him. 4 Hence, as to the eating of food offered to idols, we know that '*no idol in the world really exists,*' and that '*there is no God but one.*' 5 Indeed, even though there may be so-called gods in heaven or on earth—as in fact there are many gods and many lords—6 yet for us there is one God, the Father, from whom are all things and for whom we exist, and one Lord, Jesus Christ, through whom are all things and through whom we exist. 7 It is not everyone, however, who has this knowledge. Since some have become so accustomed to idols until now, they still think of the food they eat as food offered to an idol; and their conscience, being weak, is defiled. 8 '*Food will not bring us close to God.*' We are no worse off if we do not eat, and no better off if we do. 9 But take care that this liberty of yours does not somehow become a stumbling block to the weak. 10 For if others see you, who possess knowledge, eating

---

2. Note that in 3:16, the "you" is plural, indicating that he is referring to the church as whole, while "your body" in 6:19 is singular, referring to the individual being the temple of the Holy Spirit.

3. Mitchell, *Paul and the Rhetoric of Reconciliation*, 37–38.

in the temple of an idol, might they not, since their conscience is weak, be encouraged to the point of eating food sacrificed to idols? 11 So by your knowledge those weak believers for whom Christ died are destroyed. 12 But when you thus sin against members of your family, and wound their conscience when it is weak, you sin against Christ. 13 Therefore, if food is a cause of their falling, I will never eat meat, so that I may not cause one of them to fall."

Beginning in 1 Cor 8:1, it appears that Paul once again is responding to questions raised in the letter he received from Corinth (cf. 7:1).[4] In this text, Paul may be quoting as many as four Corinthian slogans or positions to which he wishes to respond. The first one is found in 8:1: "all of us possess knowledge." Let's examine the relative likelihood of this being a Corinthian quotation by applying our twelve steps.

Twelve Steps for Identifying Quotations: 1 Cor 8:1

1. *Context: Does the context lead us to expect a quotation?* Yes. Paul has just completed a section that began with a clear quotation using the same "now concerning" formula (7:1). The repetition of this phrase should lead us to expect that a quote may follow.

2. *Quotative Frame: Is there a "quotative frame" in the near context?* Yes. There is a verb of perception ("we know") with a ὅτι (*hoti*), translated "that," immediately preceding the potential quote.

3. *Shift in Person: Is there a shift in grammatical "person"?* Yes. There is a shift from first person ("we know") to third person ("everyone").

4. *Proverbial Statements: Is there a potential slogan in the form of a generalization, like a proverbial statement (usually expressed in the present tense)?* Perhaps, since it is brief (three words in Greek) and uses the present tense, but it does not have a proverbial ring to it.

5. *Rhetorical Features: Are there rhetorical features, such as parallel structures, that might suggest an easy to memorize catchphrase?* No.

---

4. While we have previously acknowledged Mitchell's argument ("Concerning Περὶ δέ in 1 Corinthians," 229–56) that περὶ δέ (*de*) does not *necessitate* a reference to the Corinthians' letter sent to Paul, with Thiselton (616–17) we agree that "it is virtually certain that in most cases, as here, it does serve as such a signal."

6. *Repetition: Are there expressions that are repeated at other points in the letter?* No.

7. *Diatribe: Are features of diatribe present or other rhetorical features that may suggest the presence of dialogue between the writer and others?* Yes. Earlier Paul uses the expression "do you not know" (6:2, 3, 9, 15, 16, 19; cf. 3:16; 5:6; 9:13, 24) to craft a dialogic argument, and he does the same here with "we know" in 8:1 and 8:4.

8. *Contradictions: Are there statements that appear to contradict what the author says elsewhere in the same letter?* Yes. There is an apparent contradiction between the assertion in 8:1 ("we all have knowledge") and the retort in 8:7 ("not everyone has this knowledge").

9. *Contrast: Does the writer present a sharp contrast or refutation to something he has just stated, which may have been a quotation? Or, does he make a statement and then provide commentary on that statement as if referring to something that has been expressed by others?* Yes, on both counts. "Knowledge puffs up, but love builds up" (8:1b) appears to be commentary on "we all have knowledge," while "Anyone who claims to know something does not yet have the necessary knowledge" (8:2) refutes the absolute claim that all of them possess knowledge. "Knowledge puffs up, but love builds up" also appears to be Paul's own proverbial statement, suggesting that he is playing dueling slogans once again.

10. *Common Issues: Are there expressions that may represent characteristic ways of thinking, based on the broad context of the letter, that the writer appears to be engaging with his audience?* Yes. At the very beginning of the letter Paul appears to allude, in perhaps an ironic way, to the Corinthians' infatuation with both speaking in tongues and spiritual knowledge: "I give thanks to my God always for you because of the grace of God that was given you in Christ Jesus, 5 that in every way you were enriched in him in all speech and all knowledge" (1:4–5). He later refers to the apparent view of some Corinthians that they understood "all knowledge" (13:2).

11–12. *Past Scholars and Common Sense: Is our assessment of a particular putative slogan consistent with the collective wisdom of Bible scholars and Bible translators? Does our assessment of a particular putative slogan pass the common sense test (i.e., does reading a particular text as a slogan or quotation make the best sense of the immediate context)?*

The ten translations we are considering are mixed in how they handle 8:1. Six use quotation marks to indicate Paul is quoting Corinthians (NRSV, NIV 2011, ESV, NET, MEV, and HCSB), while the other four do not (NKJV, NASB, NIV 1984, and NJB). In contrast, our commentators consistently interpret a portion of 8:1 ("we all possess knowledge") as a Corinthian slogan.[5] This is not surprising since the structure of the verse strongly implies that Paul is going to interact with something that the Corinthians had said to him in their letter.[6] Fitzmyer notes that Paul uses diatribe style in quoting a Corinthian slogan and agreeing with it in principle, before qualifying it in the following comment (vv. 1c–3b).[7] Blomberg takes a similar approach: "As with the previous slogans, there is a sense in which Paul can agree but not without immediate qualification (vv. 1b–3). Love, not knowledge, must form the foundation of Christian behavior."[8] Bruce likewise acknowledges Paul's agreement with the initial slogan, but notes that Paul is quick to remind them that "Knowledge without love—puffs up."[9]

In short, the majority of the translations we considered and a growing consensus among scholars affirm a Corinthian quotation in 8:1. Our analysis of the passage using our twelve criteria strongly supports this view.

Likelihood of a Quotation in 8:1: *Very likely.*

---

5. The only exception appears to be Taylor (204). Willis (*Idol Meat*, 68–70) argues that the full Corinthian quote includes "*we know that* all of us possess knowledge." The problem with this is that it loses its proverbial flavor and includes what appears to be a quotative frame as part of the slogan.

6. See Barrett, 189; Blomberg, 159; Conzelmann, 140; Talbert, 56.

7. Fitzmyer (338) also finds an aphoristic quality in the slogan, which he notes is another way of saying what was already said in a previous slogan in 6:12: "For me all things are permissible." Even Garland (366) acknowledges that this aphoristic quality "may suggest a slogan."

8. Blomberg, 161.

9. Bruce, 79. Hays (137) agrees with Blomberg and Bruce that Paul provisionally accepts the slogan in 8:1 that all have knowledge but "immediately suggests that knowledge is defective if it fails to build up the community in love."

The Corinthians and Community

Twelve Steps for Identifying Quotations: 1 Cor 8:4

> "Hence, as to the eating of food offered to idols, we know that 'no idol in the world really exists,' and that 'there is no God but one.'" (1 Cor 8:4)

The next possible Corinthian slogans or quotations appear in verse 4. How do our twelve criteria help us in determining whether these potential quotes are valid?

1. *Context: Does the context lead us to expect a quotation?* Yes. Paul has not only just almost certainly quoted Corinthians in 8:1, but he also introduced this passage in such a way that we expect the entire passage to be engaging Corinthian positions. Paul's use of "Now concerning" is quite likely short for "Now concerning another matter about which you wrote." It would not be surprising if Paul were to respond to multiple things that the Corinthians had said about this topic.

2. *Quotative Frame: Is there a "quotative frame" in the near context?* Yes. There is a verb of perception ("we know") with a ὅτι (*hoti*), translated "that," immediately preceding the potential quote. Even more important, this is the exact same quotative frame that Paul has just used to introduce a statement that most modern scholars agree is a quote (8:1). That quotative frame is shortened to "and that" (καὶ ὅτι, *kai hoti*) before the second possible quotation in this verse: "and that 'there is no God but one.'" This does not mean that both potential quotations come from the same source. It is quite possible that Paul first quotes the Corinthians and then quotes a common Jewish expression that was based on Deut 6:4: "Hear, O Israel: The Lord is our God, the Lord alone" (see also Mark 12:29; Gal 3:20; 1 Tim 2:5). This central declaration of faith among the people of Israel appears to have been expressed at times using the phrase "except one" in the first century (see, e.g., Mark 2:7; Mark 10:18 || Luke 18:19). Paul may have been using a quote from elsewhere to affirm the Corinthian position partially before nuancing that position. Given the way he connects them, however, both statements appear to be Corinthian quotes.[10] Beyond

---

10. They are linked with a καί (*kai*) and the second one is introduced with "that," which is clearly a shortened form of "we know that," which introduced the previous quote. Taken together, these facts point to Paul quoting Corinthians twice in this passage. The fact that he could also fully affirm at least the second quotation does not mean that it is his own statement.

all this, Paul introduces this verse with the word "concerning" (περί, *peri*), which is almost certainly an elliptical version of "now concerning," from 8:1, which is used here to indicate to the reader that Paul is restating the topic to get his argument back on track.

3. *Shift in Person: Is there a shift in grammatical "person"?* Yes. There is a shift from first person ("we know") to third person ("no idol ... exists" and "there is").

4. *Proverbial Statements: Is there a potential slogan in the form of a generalization, like a proverbial statement (usually expressed in the present tense)?* Yes, in both cases. In fact, both statements have far more of a proverbial nature in the Greek than in the NRSV: lit. "we know that 'no idol in the world' and 'no God except one'" (our translation).

5. *Rhetorical Features: Are there rhetorical features, such as parallel structures, that might suggest an easy to memorize catchphrase?* No.

6. *Repetition: Are there expressions that are repeated at other points in the letter?* Yes. There is a similar expression in 10:19, where Paul asks, "What do I imply then? That food sacrificed to idols is anything, or that *an idol is anything*?" (10:19), and then clarifies the half-truth of the Corinthian slogan by noting, "No, I imply that what pagans sacrifice, they sacrifice to demons and not to God. I do not want you to be partners with demons" (10:20). In 8:4, Paul uses the phrase, "no idol" or "nothing idol," and in 10:18, he uses the phrase, "idol anything."[11]

7. *Diatribe: Are features of diatribe present or other rhetorical features that may suggest the presence of dialogue between the writer and others?* Yes. Paul introduces the passage with "Now concerning," implying that he is going to engage in dialogue. He then makes use of "we know that" in 8:1 and twice in 8:4 (the second time with "we know" left out by ellipsis).[12]

8. *Contradictions: Are there statements that appear to contradict what the author says elsewhere in the same letter?* No.

---

11. Cf. Brookins and Longenecker (195), who translate the clause, "an idol is nothing in the world."

12. Although we do not ultimately find the conclusions of Fotopoulos convincing, his analysis does significantly support the presence of diatribe in this passage. See "Arguments Concerning Food," 611–31.

9. *Contrast: Does the writer present a sharp contrast or refutation to something he has just stated, which may have been a quotation? Or, does he make a statement and then provide commentary on that statement as if referring to something that has been expressed by others?* Yes. Paul does seem to make a statement and then offer commentary introduced with the phrase translated "Indeed, even though" by the NRSV. This expression (καὶ γὰρ εἴπερ, *kai gar eiper*) occurs only here in the New Testament. "The combined formulation [three conjunctions in a row!] substantially diminishes the legitimacy of the viewpoint that there are other entities deserving the designation 'god' or 'lord,' but the condition assumes that viewpoint for the sake of argument."[13] While there appears to be a strong contrast introduced in verse 6 with the conjunction ἀλλά (*alla*; NRSV: "yet"), two factors need to be noted. First, if there is a strong contrast, Paul is contrasting what follows with his own statement that precedes in verse 5, rather than with the possible Corinthian quote in verse 4. Second, "After ἐὰν [*ean*], ἀλλά [*alla*] does not introduce simple contrast but rather adds an additional consideration; thus 'still' (cf. BDAG, 45.4.a)."[14] Therefore, we find commentary, but not strong refutation of a putative quote at this point in the passage making the evidence from this criterion relatively weak.

10. *Common Issues: Are there expressions that may represent characteristic ways of thinking, based on the broad context of the letter, that the writer appears to be engaging with his audience?* Yes. As we have already noted, Paul engages apparent Corinthian claims to knowledge in this letter. He also engages problems in the church related to food offered to idols. Here, those two issues may well come together, with the Corinthians asserting their possession of the knowledge that idols are nothing, which in turn leads them not to be concerned about eating food that has been offered to idols/nothing.

11–12. *Past Scholars and Common Sense: Is our assessment of a particular putative slogan consistent with the collective wisdom of Bible scholars and Bible translators? Does our assessment of a particular putative slogan pass the common sense test (i.e., does reading a particular text as a slogan or quotation make the best sense of the immediate context)?*

---

13. Brookins and Longenecker, 196.
14. Ibid., 111.

Five of our translations include quotation marks with both potential quotations in 8:4 (NET, NRSV, NIV 2011, ESV, and HCSB), and five do not use quotation marks with either expression (NKJV, NASB, NIV 1984, MEV, and NJB). Notably, the MEV acknowledges a quotation in 8:1, but not here. Among our fifteen scholars, Blomberg does not point to a Corinthian quotation here.[15] Garland appears to prefer the view that no Corinthian slogan is in view, while acknowledging that "Paul may be quoting a line from the Corinthians' letter."[16] He goes on to note that "If so, they were simply parroting what they would have heard from Paul's first preaching (cf. Gal. 4:8)."[17] Fee, Hays, Conzelmann, Fitzmyer, Taylor, Brookins/Longenecker, Ciampa/Rosner, and Bruce, on the other hand, maintain that Paul is quoting Corinthians twice in verse 4.[18] Conzelmann argues that the two Corinthian slogans found in 8:4 provide the "theoretical foundation for the practice of freedom" to which Paul will respond.[19] Keener affirms that in 8:4 "Paul summarizes their own position (or a useful insight in it) as he sees it, then refutes or qualifies it."[20]

Witherington, on the other hand, maintains that what the NRSV presents as two quotations is really a single Corinthian quotation.[21] Thiselton appears to take the same view, but is also somewhat sympathetic with the view of Willis, who treats verses 4b-6 as an extended Corinthian assertion.[22] Talbert posits that the Corinthians have been making two claims ("no idol in the world really exists," and "there is no God but one") and supporting those claims with an appeal to a creedal statement, which Paul reproduces

---

15. Although Blomberg argues (161–62) that the declaration of the existence of only one true God in the universe is from Paul and not the Corinthians (v. 4), he acknowledges that some Corinthian Christians were perhaps using this logic to justify their freedom to eat.

16. Garland, 371.

17. Ibid.

18. Fee, 370; Hays, 138–39; Conzelmann, 142; Fitzmyer, 340; Bruce, 80; Taylor, 205; Brookins and Longenecker, 192–93; Ciampa and Rosner, 379. Fee notes elsewhere (365) that "when Paul is expressing his own ideas he never repeats with a ὅτι [hoti]," thus making it more likely that Paul is referring to the Corinthians' affirmation of the monotheistic creed in verse 4, an affirmation that he himself could also make.

19. Conzelmann, 140.

20. Keener, 73.

21. Witherington, 188. Barrett (191) appears to also attribute both quotations to the Corinthians, though his position is not clear.

22. Thiselton, 631.

in verses 5–6.[23] Since these arguments will take us into new territory of considering the possibility that Paul is citing an extended Corinthian quotation, we will come back to them below. For now, we will simply note that of the commentaries we are considering Blomberg is the only commentator who seems to indicate that the statement in 8:4 belongs to Paul. If we take the two statements in 8:4 as Paul quoting Corinthians, on the other hand, what follows makes very good sense as Paul's response to those statements. He first agrees with their monotheistic declaration (vv. 5–6), relegating idols to "so-called gods" (v. 5), and then proceeds to remind them that their lifestyles must also recognize that "not everyone . . . has this knowledge" (v. 7). Combined with the rest of our criteria, we have strong evidence for Paul quoting Corinthians here.

Likelihood of a Quotation in 8:4: *Very likely* for both 8:4a and 8:4b.

Twelve Steps for Identifying Quotations: 1 Cor 8:8

> "'Food will not bring us close to God.' We are no worse off if we do not eat, and no better off if we do." (1 Cor 8:8)

The next possible Corinthian slogan we will consider appears in verse 8. Although we are getting ahead of ourselves, it is worth noting at this point that of our ten translations *only* the NRSV uses quotation marks in this verse. Let's examine how the potential quote fares when our criteria are applied.

1. *Context: Does the context lead us to expect a quotation?* Perhaps. The passage already appears to make use of three Corinthian quotations, with the last one coming in verse 4.
2. *Quotative Frame: Is there a "quotative frame" in the near context?* No. There is no formal indication in the Greek that a quote will follow. This is important, since the earlier putative quotations in this passage each involve a quotative frame.
3. *Shift in Person: Is there a shift in grammatical "person"?* Yes. Although Paul has been speaking in the third person, and he continues to do so, there is a shift after the putative quote to the first person ("We are

23. Talbert, 57.

no worse off," v. 8b) or the second person "But [you] take care," v. 9), either of which could mark the end of the quotation.

4. *Proverbial Statements: Is there a potential slogan in the form of a generalization, like a proverbial statement (usually expressed in the present tense)?* Perhaps, but not likely. The statement reads like a typical statement. The fact that it includes the conjunction δέ (*de*) seems to mark it as the next step in Paul's argument, rather than a Corinthian quotation.

5. *Rhetorical Features: Are there rhetorical features, such as parallel structures, that might suggest an easy to memorize catchphrase?* No. The following statement includes parallel structures, but this one does not. This could suggest that the entire verse is a Corinthian quote, but such a lengthy quote is unlikely without some sort of formal marker (e.g., a quotative frame).

6. *Repetition: Are there expressions that are repeated at other points in the letter?* No.

7. *Diatribe: Are features of diatribe present or other rhetorical features that may suggest the presence of dialogue between the writer and others?* Yes. We have already seen extensive features of diatribe in this passage, but there are no clear features of diatribe in the immediate context.

8. *Contradictions: Are there statements that appear to contradict what the author says elsewhere in the same letter?* Yes. If 8:8 is taken to mean, either in whole or in part, that it simply does not matter what one eats, then we have an apparent contradiction with what Paul himself clearly asserts in 11:20–22. What followers of Jesus eat *does* matter, because they dare not provoke the Lord to jealousy by presuming to partake of both the Lord's Table and the table of demons.

9. *Contrast: Does the writer present a sharp contrast or refutation to something he has just stated, which may have been a quotation? Or, does he make a statement and then provide commentary on that statement as if referring to something that has been expressed by others?* No. There is no clear refutation; but 8:9 does appear to be commentary on the statement made in 8:8.

10. *Common Issues: Are there expressions that may represent characteristic ways of thinking, based on the broad context of the letter, that the writer appears to be engaging with his audience?* Yes. The putative quotes

seem to reflect the wrong-headed distinction the Corinthians had drawn between the material world and the spiritual realm. If 8:8a is read as a quote, the Corinthians are essentially again asserting that physical things (in this case food) are simply not relevant now.

11–12. *Past Scholars and Common Sense: Is our assessment of a particular putative slogan consistent with the collective wisdom of Bible scholars and Bible translators? Does our assessment of a particular putative slogan pass the common sense test (i.e., does reading a particular text as a slogan or quotation make the best sense of the immediate context)?*

None of our ten translations use quotation marks in this verse with the exception of the NRSV, which marks "Food will not bring us close to God" as a quotation and includes a footnote indicating that "the quotation may extend to the end of the verse."[24] If 8:8 does include a quotation, with either one or two statements from the Corinthians, then the dialogue it presents would look like this:

> *The Corinthians Assertion:* "Food will not bring us close to God. [We are no worse off if we do not eat, and no better off if we do.]"
>
> *Paul's Response:* "But take care that this liberty of yours does not somehow become a stumbling block to the weak..."

When we move to our commentaries we find far more support for Corinthian quotations in this verse than our English translations indicate. Hays treats 8:8a as a Corinthian quote, as do Thiselton, Talbert, and Brookins/Longenecker.[25] Witherington views both 8:8a and 8:8b as Corinthian quotes, as does Fitzmyer and Ciampa/Rosner, while Keener and Taylor are at least open to the possibility of all of 8:8 being a Corinthian quote.[26] Fitzmyer bases his position on the shift from the third person plural used by Paul in 8:7 to the first person plural in 8:8b, which he views as evidence that the whole of 8:8 is likely a Corinthian slogan.[27] Interpreted in this way, 8:8 reflects the view that some Corinthians possess the specific knowledge

---

24. Note the theological similarities between this statement and the assertion made by the Corinthians in 6:12–13.

25. Hays, 141; Thiselton, 647; Talbert, 58; Brookins and Longenecker, 198–200.

26. Witherington, 199; Fitzmyer, 345; Keener, 73; Ciampa and Rosner, 388–89; Taylor, 207.

27. Fitzmyer, 345. It then "reads like a protest from them and may be another way of phrasing the slogan about food in 6:13" (ibid).

(8:1) that there is no danger of incurring the wrath of God because of eating idol meat. Verse 9, which shifts back to the second person plural, would then serve as Paul's response to the "in the know" Corinthians. Bruce states that 8:8a "may also be a quotation from the Corinthian letter."[28] Barrett tacitly affirms that Paul is stating the Corinthian position.[29] Garland recognizes that Paul is engaging a Corinthian position but does not address the question of whether or not a quotation is involved.[30] Fee states that "both sentences reflect what the Corinthians were arguing in their letter, whether they are direct quotations or not."[31] He goes on to suggest that "The reason for the lack of quotation marks [in his translation] is that they also fully accord with Paul's own point of view."[32]

Part of the challenge in evaluating the quotation in 8:8 is the question of what the verb (παραστήσει, *parastēsei*), translated "bring us close" by the NRSV, actually means. While the NRSV leaves the impression that food simply does not help us to have a closer relationship with God, Garland argues that "Since Paul also uses the future tense of the verb in Rom. 14:10 with the idea of standing before God's judgment seat . . . it may have that same connotation here."[33] In that case, the idea would be that "Food is an indifferent matter that will not bring us before the Judge for condemnation."[34]

---

28. Bruce, 81.
29. Barrett, 195.
30. Garland, 379, 385.
31. Fee, 383.
32. Ibid. Fee also notes (384) the parallelism between what Paul says about food in 8:8b and the almost exact argument he makes elsewhere about circumcision (7:19; Gal 5:6; 6:15). With Witherington, he posits that 8:8b "very likely reflects Paul's own position on being 'kosher,' that food, like circumcision, does not 'present us' to God. We are none the worse if we do not eat such food (as with not being circumcised) and we are no better if we do (as with being circumcised). Such are strictly matters of indifference to God." Conzelmann's view on this passage is not clear.
33. Garland, 385.
34. Ibid. Garland's argument, however, needs to be nuanced because although both verbs are future tense, the verb παραστήσει (*parastēsei*) is used intransitively in Rom 14:10 (in the middle voice), making translations like "appear" or "stand" plausible, but in 1 Cor 8:8 Paul uses the verb transitively (i.e., with a direct object). In other words, in 1 Cor 8:8, this verb is indicating what food *does to us*, rather than indicating something that *we do*, as in Romans. Brookins and Longenecker (200) maintain that "The meaning, as Robertson-Plummer (170) note, is '[will not] present for approbation or condemnation,' with approbation being foremost in Paul's mind. Accordingly, the future tense probably points to the final judgment." Indeed, it may well be used as a legal technical term here to indicate "bring before (a judge)" (BDAG, 778.1.e).

This certainly makes good sense of the context. The Corinthians would be asserting that they can eat whatever they want because it will have no spiritual ramifications whatsoever. God is not going to judge anyone based on the food on their plate.

Blomberg and Conzelmann are the only commentators we reviewed who explicitly reject a Corinthian slogan in 8:8. Blomberg believes that the introductory "but" in 8:8a should be translated "and," with the whole of 8:8 continuing Paul's qualification on Christian freedom that he began in 8:7.[35] Although Blomberg offers no justification for his preference, as we noted above the conjunction δέ (*de*) that Paul uses here naturally points toward the next development in *Paul's* argument. Read in this manner, Paul himself is emphasizing the moral neutrality of sacrificial food first by a brief general statement (8:8a) and then by an elaborative statement in 8:8b. Thus, Paul responds in 8:7–9 to the Corinthians' boast that their knowledge of the truth leads them to enjoy freedom in eating all food by first agreeing with the basis for that boast (food has no bearing on our relationship with God), but then qualifying that general principle by appealing to the needs of others. As Conzelmann likewise notes, "the neutrality of food does *not* mean neutrality of *conduct*."[36]

So, where does common sense play into our analysis of this passage? The position that Paul is quoting Corinthians here is not helped by the fact that there are no explicit markers (a Quotative Frame). As we noted earlier in our study, however, Paul clearly does not always include formal markers when introducing quotations, even when they are from the Old Testament. Thus, we must look to our other criteria and the preponderance of evidence. Although we could make sense of 8:8 if Paul were quoting Corinthians in either the first part of the verse or the verse as a whole, our twelve-step process suggests that there are not sufficient clues to recognize a quotation here, and 8:8a does not have the characteristics of a slogan. Particularly overlooked is the fact that the conjunction Paul uses to introduce 8:8 likely marks it as the next development in his argument. The beginning of 8:8 is, therefore, appropriately translated: "*Now*, food will not bring us before God (to judge us) . . ."[37]

---

35. Blomberg, 162.

36. Conzelmann, 148.

37. Although none of our translations contain quotation marks in 8:9–10, Omanson ("Acknowledging Paul's Quotations," 210) suggests that Paul may be utilizing additional Corinthian words and phrases in these verses. The word "liberty" nicely captures the attitude of many Corinthians toward various issues, including eating food sacrificed

Likelihood: *Unlikely, but possible.*

An Extended Quotation in 8:4–6?

Our discussion of 8:8 helps to highlight one final important question in this passage. As mentioned above, Talbert and others have suggested that there is actually an extended quotation of the Corinthians in 8:4–6. In this view, which follows Willis, Paul does not respond to the Corinthian position until 8:7.[38] Instead, he cites two Corinthian slogans along with the Corinthians' supporting arguments from their letter before proceeding to offer his own response beginning in verse 7:

> *The Corinthian Assertion:* "We know that no idol in the world really exists, and that there is no God but one."
>
> *The Corinthians' supporting appeal to creedal statements:* "Indeed, even though there may be so-called gods in heaven or on earth—as in fact there are many gods and many lords—yet for us there is one God, the Father, from whom are all things and for whom we exist, and one Lord, Jesus Christ, through whom are all things and through whom we exist."
>
> *Paul's Response:* "It is not everyone, however, who has this knowledge . . .'"

The question of an extended quotation takes us into new territory. It is easier to posit a Corinthian quotation when we are dealing with likely slogans. On what basis, though, can we, with any level of confidence, identify an extended quotation when Greek writers did not use quotation marks? To do so, we will need some criteria to supplement our twelve steps. Before considering new criteria, however, we need to recognize the fact that 1 Corinthians clearly indicates, at times, that Paul is referring back to what

---

to idols. Fee (384–85) thus argues that Paul is using the Corinthian's own catchwords against them in 8:9–10 in a sarcastic manner: "But take care that this 'freedom' of yours . . ." The Good News Bible follows this interpretation and thus translates the first part of 8:10: "Suppose a person whose conscience is weak in this matter sees you, who have so-called 'knowledge . . .'"

38. Willis (*Idol Meat*, 85–86; cf. Thiselton, 631) and some others who take this view have maintained that "as in fact there are many gods and many lords" (v. 5b) is Paul's own parenthetical comment. Others reject this analysis; see, e.g., Fee, 371n10; Hays, 139; Conzelmann, 144.

the Corinthians have said to him in their letter(s). This is indisputable; and it makes it quite plausible, *prima facie*, that Paul would quote not only Corinthians slogans, but also more extended statements from the Corinthians' letter. How can we test putative extended quotations? We suggest the addition of four supplemental criteria, the first of which is closely connected to an earlier criterion.

Supplemental Criteria for Identifying Extended Quotations

(1) *Initial Quotative Frame: Is there an initial quotative frame that may introduce an extended quotation?* In our view, the presence of a quotative frame is far more important if we are going to have any textual basis for an *extended* quotation. Although it is logical to assume that the Corinthians would quickly recognize when Paul was quoting their letter, two factors need to be kept in mind. First, we are likely not dealing with a single house church in Corinth. At the very least, it is unlikely that if a certain faction wrote to Paul, everyone in the church in Corinth was aware of the precise contents of that letter. Second, Paul explicitly addresses his letter not only to the church in Corinth, but also to "all those who in every place call on the name of our Lord Jesus Christ" (1:2). There is no way that he could expect believers in other cities to be familiar with the contents of a letter the Corinthians had sent to him. He would, therefore, need to somehow mark Corinthian quotations if they were not clearly slogan-like in nature. In the case of 8:4–6, we have a quotative frame of sorts at the beginning of the putative extended quotation: "we know that" (8:4).

(2) *Grammatical Extension: Is there grammatical evidence for an extension of the initial quote?* The point with this criterion, like the last one, is to expect explicit markers in the language the writer has chosen to point to an extended quotation. Perhaps the most natural way of doing this is through the use of "For" (γάρ, *gar*). "The presence of γάρ constrains the material that it introduces to be interpreted as *strengthening* some aspect of the previous assertion, rather than as distinctive information."[39] Similarly, Stephanie Black notes that "Γάρ [*gar*] is used to direct the audience to strengthen the preceding proposition,

---

39. Levinsohn, *Discourse Features*, 92; see also Runge, *Discourse Grammar*, 52; Heckert, *Discourse Function*, 31, 36.

confirming it as part of the mental representation they construct of the discourse."[40] The question this leaves us, of course, is whether Paul is introducing material to strengthen the position stated in the Corinthian quotation(s), or whether this reflects the Corinthians' effort to strengthen their position introduced in verse 4. Verse 5 is, in fact, introduced with a γάρ (*gar*, "for"), which the NRSV apparently translates "Indeed," while many other English versions use the more common "For" (e.g., NASB, NIV, RSV, HCSB, MEV). The use of this conjunction makes it plausible that Paul's quotation of the Corinthians extends all the way through verse 6, since verses 5–6 form a single sentence.

(3) *Delayed Response: Is there evidence that Paul's response (commentary or contrast or refutation) might be delayed?* Yes. We get a strong contrast introduced in verse 7 using the conjunction ἀλλά (*alla*, "but"; NRSV: "however"). Although there is also a strong contrast introduced in verse 6 through the use of the conjunction ἀλλά (*alla*, "but"; NRSV: "yet"), that contrast is clearly part of a sentence introduced in verse 5, which may well be the Corinthians' statement. It is thus grammatically plausible that Paul's refutation of the Corinthian position does not begin until verse 7.

(4) *The Writer's Voice: Is there evidence within the putative extended quote that it is the writer's own voice rather than a quotation?* Does the *entire* putative extended quotation make good sense as the words of someone else, or are there portions that strongly appear to reflect the writer's own words? There are a couple of points in the verses in question where it makes more sense to read Paul as the speaker than the Corinthians. First, the parenthetical statement in verse 5 ("as in fact there are many gods and many lords") seems to make better sense as Paul's observation, though it could also fit as part of an extended Corinthian quote. More important, both the "yet for us" and particularly the rich theological content that follows appears to come from Paul rather than the theologically impoverished Corinthians.

Where does that leave us? Although the cumulative weight of evidence could suggest that verses 4–6 are an extended Corinthian quotation, they more likely represent two brief Corinthian quotations (v. 4) followed by Paul's own reflections on their position (vv. 5–6), which in turn is followed

---

40. Black, *Sentence Conjunctions*, 280; cited in Runge, *Discourse Grammar*, 52.

by his commentary on the Corinthian position (vv. 7–13). The expression "we know that" (οἴδαμεν ὅτι, *oidamen hoti*) appears to be Paul's own words, which introduce the Corinthians' statements and in this case communicate that which Paul and the Corinthians agree upon. Even though the agreed upon principles, likely stated as Corinthian quotations (v. 4), are expanded upon in verses 5–6, that expansion appears more likely to represent Paul's words rather than the Corinthians'.[41]

Theological Implications

The issue that Paul is addressing in this part of 1 Corinthians revolves around a situation in which members of the Corinthian church who deemed themselves to be enlightened with spiritual knowledge had been partaking of food that had been offered to idols. Paul, however, notes that others within the community who do not possess this knowledge have been influenced by their behavior and have also been consuming food dedicated to idols, which has hurt their consciences. The "strong" were boasting of their freedom to eat such food, knowing that pagan deities do not really exist. Unfortunately, the weaker members of the church did not recognize this truth (8:8). This is Paul's concern. And he, therefore, warned the Corinthians that by exercising their freedom the "strong" were actually sinning against their "weaker" brothers and sisters in the Lord, which in turn means they were sinning against Christ (8:12). Life is not about individual

---

41. Fotopoulos sees far more back and forth between Paul and the Corinthians in 8:1–9 ("Arguments Concerning Food," 611–31). He reconstructs the dialogue as follows. "*Strong's Quotation*: We know that we all have knowledge. *Paul's Refutation*: Knowledge puffs up, but love builds up. If someone thinks to know something, one does not yet know as one should know. But if someone loves God, that one is known by him. *Strong's Quotation*: We know that no idol exists in the world and that no God exists but one. For even if there are so-called gods, whether in heaven or whether on earth . . . *Paul's Refutation*: As in fact there are many gods and many lords. *Strong's Quotation*: But for us there is one God, the Father, from whom are all things and for whom we exist, and there is one Lord, Jesus Christ, through whom are all things and through whom we exist. *Paul's Refutation*: But not everyone has this knowledge. Since some are so accustomed to idols until now, they eat this food as food offered to idols and their moral consciousness, being weak, is defiled. *Strong's Quotation*: Food will not bring us before the judgment of God. We are worse off if we do not eat, and we are better off if we eat. *Paul's Refutation*: We are no worse off if we do not eat, and we are not better off if we eat. Beware that this liberty of yours does not become a stumbling block to the Weak." While this analysis is fascinating, we believe it is ultimately untenable given the lack of explicit indicators in the text that such a dialogue is in view (cf. our analysis of 8:5–6 above).

freedom; it is about the glory of God and the good of God's people. Therefore, Paul concludes: "if food is a cause of their falling, I will never eat meat so that I may not cause one of them to fall" (8:13). Paul's application in this final verse parallels the principle he articulated in 8:1, which should govern all Christian decisions: "love builds up."

As we look at the Corinthian slogans Paul chose to quote, we find an important lesson for followers of Jesus throughout the ages. Paul argues that the actions of some Corinthians, which were based on their spiritual knowledge (8:1), were actually destructive, rather than edifying for the church. They rightly recognized that there is only one God and that idols are really nothing at all. Paul *agrees* with this assessment and he makes that clear in 8:5–6.[42] Therefore, Paul concedes, all things being equal it is fine to eat meat that had been dedicated to lifeless idols (8:4–5). After all, God is not going to hold his people accountable based on what they eat. Paul agrees with the Corinthians that "Food will not bring us close to God," by himself affirming, "We are no worse off if we do not eat, and no better off if we do" (8:8). But that is not the end of the story.

The Corinthians have got their theology right, Paul affirms; but they have failed in properly *applying* that theology to life. These "knowledgeable" believers are not considering the impact that their actions are having upon other believers. As Keener notes,

> even if idols were nothing, Paul points out, those who fail to share this conviction nevertheless participate in idolatry against their own faith when they eat idol food (8:7). Because idol food holds a different social and theological significance for the 'weak' . . . they may follow the example of the 'liberated' in a way that compromises their own monotheism.[43]

Like the Corinthians, followers of Jesus can easily fall into the trap of living their lives in light of the sure knowledge of the freedom they have in their relationship with God, not recognizing that their exercise of those freedoms can hurt less mature believers. This is dangerous. Those who follow Jesus should be eager to do everything they can to avoid having the

---

42. This is likely true whether or not vv. 5–6 represent an extended quotation. Hays (138–39) rightly points out that "even more clearly than in the previous cases, these slogans express a theological perspective with which Paul does not disagree; his quarrel is with the Corinthians' *application* of the slogans. Because the idol has no real existence, they contend, idol worship is a meaningless gesture."

43. Keener, 74.

proverbial millstone hung around their neck and then being launched into the sea (see Luke 17:2). Ultimately, Paul argues that love must limit liberty when it comes to keeping a fellow believer from stumbling.[44]

What does this look like? I (Martin) remember years ago living in a small town across the street from an elderly woman who was always careful to avoid any kind of work on Sunday. She had grown up in a very conservative family and had a deep desire to please the Lord in all things. Personally, I did not believe that the Bible prohibited me from mowing my lawn on Sunday; but I knew that if I chose to do so, I could easily lead my neighbor to do something on Sunday that was against her conscience. What was the answer? Limit my freedom to help ensure the good of my neighbor. Being able to do what I wanted was not what was important. Love was what was important.

Twelve Steps for Identifying Quotations: 1 Cor 10:23

> "'All things are lawful,' but not all things are beneficial. 'All things are lawful,' but not all things build up."

Paul's instructions regarding eating food that has been sacrificed to idols does not end in 1 Cor 8. He addresses the same issue head on in 1 Cor 10. Once again, he appears to use a slogan to help make his point; and in this case it is the same exact expression that he used in 6:12. Let's apply our twelve criteria to this passage to determine the likelihood of slogans here.

1. *Context: Does the context lead us to expect a quotation?* No. There are not strong contextual indicators that a quote should be expected.

2. *Quotative Frame: Is there a "quotative frame" in the near context?* No.

3. *Shift in Person: Is there a shift in grammatical "person"?* Yes. Paul moves from first person "are *we* provoking ... Are *we* stronger" to third person "All things are lawful" to second person "Do not seek your own advantage." In 10:21, Paul had shifted for a moment to second person address ("You cannot drink the cup of the Lord and the cup of

---

44. Witherington (199) calls this "the stumbling block principle," which should be utilized to guide "one's actions in cases with no clear right and wrong, that is, in *adiaphora*." Note the many theological parallels found in Rom 14:1—15:7, especially Paul's words in 14:20–21: "Do not, for the sake of food, destroy the work of God. Everything is indeed clean, but it is wrong for you to make others fall by what you eat; it is good not to eat meat or drink wine or do anything that makes your brother or sister stumble."

demons. You cannot partake of the table of the Lord and the table of demons") followed by first person address with a rhetorical question ("Or are we provoking the Lord to jealousy? Are we stronger than he?"). It would be natural to follow this with Corinthian positions that may provoke the Lord to jealousy.

4. *Proverbial Statements: Is there a potential slogan in the form of a generalization, like a proverbial statement (usually expressed in the present tense)?* Yes.

5. *Rhetorical Features: Are there rhetorical features, such as parallel structures, that might suggest an easy to memorize catchphrase?* Yes. Paul has once again clearly made use of a parallel structure:

   "All things are lawful"
   But not all things are beneficial
   "All things are lawful"
   But not all things build up

6. *Repetition: Are there expressions that are repeated at other points in the letter?* Yes. The fact that Paul uses the exact same clause twice in the same verse increases the likelihood that he is quoting Corinthians here. The fact that he uses the same statement twice in quick succession earlier in the letter (see 6:12) is strong evidence for a quotation both here and there.

7. *Diatribe: Are features of diatribe present or other rhetorical features that may suggest the presence of dialogue between the writer and others?* Yes. The extensive use of rhetorical questions in the preceding context points to the dialogic style that was characteristic of diatribe.

8. *Contradictions: Are there statements that appear to contradict what the author says elsewhere in the same letter?* Yes. Throughout the letter, Paul has been urging the Corinthians to change their behavior. For Paul himself to say that "All things are lawful" would appear to be a contradiction.

9. *Contrast: Does the writer present a sharp contrast or refutation to something he has just stated, which may have been a quotation? Or, does he make a statement and then provide commentary on that statement as if referring to something that has been expressed by others?* Yes. Paul

introduces strong contrasts to both statements introduced with the conjunction ἀλλά (*alla*, "but").

10. *Common Issues: Are there expressions that may represent characteristic ways of thinking, based on the broad context of the letter, that the writer appears to be engaging with his audience?* Yes. The letter reveals a strong individualistic, self-seeking attitude among the Corinthians. This is revealed in their sexual pursuits, their willingness to take other believers to court, their commitment to eating food that had been sacrificed to idols regardless of how it impacted fellow believers, and so forth. This "I can do whatever I please" attitude toward life is nicely captured in the saying, "All things are lawful."

11–12. *Past Scholars and Common Sense: Is our assessment of a particular putative slogan consistent with the collective wisdom of Bible scholars and Bible translators? Does our assessment of a particular putative slogan pass the common sense test (i.e., does reading a particular text as a slogan or quotation make the best sense of the immediate context)?*

Neither the NKJV nor the NASB use quotation marks at all in this verse, leaving the impression that Paul is stating his own view that Christians have freedom to choose to do whatever they wish, but nevertheless warns of the need to consider the edification of others when making choices (10:29). The vast majority of translations (NRSV, NIV 1984, NIV 2011, ESV, NET, MEV, HCSB, and NJB), however, use quotation marks in this verse. Some translations attempt to make the source of the quotation explicit by adding the words "you say," which are not present in the Greek: "'I have the right to do anything,' you say—but not everything is beneficial" (NIV 2011). Indeed, Omanson argues that "the best translation is probably one which inserts the words 'Some of you say.'"[45] Of special note is the NJB, which includes quotation marks in 10:23a, but not in 10:23b: "'Everything is permissible'; maybe so, but not everything does good. True, everything is permissible, but not everything builds people up." Although the NJB omits quotation marks in 10:23b, it is implied that Paul is referring to the Corinthians' position a second time. At any rate, the consensus among translations is that Paul is quoting Corinthians here.

Likewise, most scholars argue that 10:23 contains a specific Corinthian slogan that Paul is quoting. Out of the fifteen commentaries we are considering, only Keener did not clearly indicate that Paul was quoting an

---

45. Omanson, "Acknowledging Paul's Quotations," 210.

actual slogan of his opponents, though he acknowledges that Paul was using elements of diatribe in his argument, and his affirmation of a slogan here is implied by his treatment of 6:12.[46]

Most scholars deal with 10:23 in basically the same way that they dealt with 6:12, where the same apparent slogan is used twice. Blomberg notes that 10:23 is stated almost verbatim from 6:12, with the primary difference being Paul's response to the slogan. This is driven by the fact that Paul's concern here is more on "the corporate than of the individual effects of exercising freedom in Christ. Still, his 'Yes, but' approach to the Corinthian slogans remains unchanged."[47] Hays agrees and also notes that Paul's divergence from his pattern in 6:12 by writing, "not all things build up," rather than, "I will not be dominated by anything," allows him to signal "that he is reaching the conclusion of his treatment of idol food, which began in 8:1 with the declaration that 'love builds up.'"[48] In the end, acknowledging that Paul is quoting Corinthians here results in a text that smoothly shifts back and forth between the Corinthians' position and Paul's position and sets up Paul's final climactic thoughts on matters of freedom in verses 24-33.

Likelihood of a Quotation in 10:23: *Very Likely.*

---

46. Keener, 57, 89.
47. Blomberg, 202.
48. Hays, 175; so also Fee, 476. Fitzmyer (397-98) notes the broader parallels in vocabulary between this passage and 8:1-13, such as "edify," "conscience," and "offense."
49. The material here builds heavily on Talbert, *Romans*, 312-16.
50. Ibid., 312.
51. Ibid., 318.

A CLOSER LOOK[49]

Romans 14:1—15:13: Issues of *Adiaphora*

Romans 14:1–15:13 has many similarities with 1 Cor 8–10, with Paul appearing to rework the same material and apply it to new circumstances in 1 Corinthians.[50] His concern is with "matters of indifference," otherwise known as *adiaphora*. Paul recognizes that there are things that are biblically neutral. This was not a new concept, but was well known among Stoic philosophers. Epictetus (*Dissertations* 2.19.13) wrote that "Virtues and the things that go along with them are good. Vices and the things that go along with vices are bad. But the things that come between these are indifferent (*adiaphora*)" (our translation). Paul seems to place dietary issues and the observance of special days in the category of *adiaphora* for followers of Jesus, but he recognizes with Epictetus that how such matters are dealt with in practice is quite important (see *Dissertations* 2.5.7). For Paul, it was critical that *adiaphora* not lead to division. As things stood, on the one hand, the "weak" were judging some members of the congregation in Rome as deficient in their faith because of their eating practices. For them, eating the right food was an essential mark of the people of God. On the other hand, some of the "strong" in Rome were putting their private freedom ahead of everything else, including the welfare of the "weak."

How did Paul deal with the problem in Romans? Romans 14:1–12 corrects both the weak and the strong, and urges Christians to avoid judging one another in matters of indifference (*adiaphora*). Romans 14:13–23 urges the strong not to become stumbling blocks to the weak. Paul agreed with their theological stance: "I know and am persuaded in the Lord Jesus that nothing is unclean in itself, but it is unclean for anyone who thinks it is unclean" (14:14). The "strong," like Paul, understood that they were dealing with *adiaphora*, but there was still significant danger in how they applied that knowledge. So Paul urgently warns them, "do not let what you regard as good [your knowledge that nothing is unclean in itself and we thus have freedom to eat anything] be spoken of as evil" (14:16). He goes on to tell them, "it is wrong for you to make others fall by what you eat" (14:20).

As Talbert notes, Martin Luther's words (*The Freedom of a Christian*, 344) nicely sum up what Paul is saying in this passage: "A Christian is a perfectly free lord of all, subject to none. A Christian is a perfectly dutiful servant, subject to all."[51] In other words, love for their brothers and sisters is what must dictate the behavior of followers of Christ, not simply a proper sense of Christian liberty. Such love will lead to mutual acceptance rather than division when dealing with *adiaphora*. Diversity is not something to be avoided. Given the different speeds at which genuine Christians grow in their faith, diversity is inevitable. The key is to promote harmony within diversity by distinguishing theological non-negotiables from theological *adiaphora*.

For Christians today, that means asking: What are points of dispute among Christians today that could be "matters of indifference," rather than essentials of the faith? How should these be handled? Will Christians insist on their personal freedom in such cases or work for harmony and edification among God's people?

Theological Implications

It is quite possible that the slogan in 10:23 developed as a summary of how the Corinthians understood Paul's own teaching, which he expressed in writing in a later letter: "Now the Lord is the Spirit, and where the Spirit of the Lord is, there is freedom" (2 Cor 3:17). If so, some within the church were taking Paul's teachings out of context, or at least extending them to a conclusion he never intended. Paul's gospel of freedom was a message of freedom from the law of sin and death through Jesus Christ (see, e.g., Rom 8:1–4). Some among his readers had twisted this so that it became a license for living however they wanted.

In this text, Paul is grappling with issues about freedom within the community that he began in 8:1 and completes at the end of 1 Cor 10 (or in 11:1). In this final portion of Paul's extended argument, he repeats a quotation from some of the Corinthians that he had cited earlier in 6:12. Though Paul's citation of the slogan is almost identical in these two passages, in 10:23 he is developing his argument in such a way as to emphasize the need to build up the community by arguing that Christians should not merely seek out things that they may be *permitted* to do, but rather, they should be concerned with what edifies God's people.

For Paul, the real issues are deeper than the mere question of what food one eats, and they reveal larger problems that have led to the divisions that have plagued the church in Corinth (cf. 1:10–11; 3:3; 11:18–19). Paul, therefore, appeals to the Corinthians to seek "the advantage" of the church as a whole when considering how to conduct themselves.[52] This corporate emphasis is captured in Thiselton's translation: "'Liberty to do all things,' but not everything is helpful. 'The right to do anything,' but not everything builds up [the church]."[53] Paul's qualification of the Corinthian slogan clearly emphasizes that unrestrained freedom will not promote the building up of the church, which should be the primary concern of followers of Jesus. To drive this point home, Paul makes use of the common rhetorical "appeal to advantage" in 10:24 with his imperative: "do not seek your own advantage, but that of the other."

The astute reader would certainly hear Paul's own story in his rebuttal to the church. Paul's apostleship was characterized by surrendering his

---

52. See Mackie, "The Two Tables," 317–31; and Mitchell, *Paul and the Rhetoric of Reconciliation*, 25–39, 256–58.

53. Thiselton, 779. It would be, of course, preferable for a translation to be consistent in translating the same Greek expression both times it occurs.

rights for the advantage of others. He had already emphasized this earlier in this section of 1 Corinthians: "though I am free with respect to all, I have made myself a slave to all, so that I might win more of them" (9:19). His selfless example, which has led to great benefit for the Corinthians, should motivate them to be willing to sacrifice their rights for the community's advantage, including those who are "weak." He uses his own example and an "appeal to advantage" once more in 10:33: "just as I try to please everyone in everything I do, not seeking my own advantage, but that of many, so that they may be saved" (10:33). To this he adds a final exhortation, "be imitators of me, as I am of Christ" (11:1), making the personal application he is calling for patently obvious. Just as Paul's example of surrendering personal rights for the sake of the church was modeled after Christ's self-sacrifice for others (see Phil 2:5–11), so each member of the church should be willing to give up his or her rights for the benefit of the community.[54]

---

54. "Paul's demonstration of how this axiom should operate at Corinth has been set forth in 8:7–13, where concern for the brother or sister for whom Christ died takes priority over one's own concerns for self-affirmation, self-gratification, or self-fulfillment" (Ciampa and Rosner, 486).

9

The Corinthians and Order

Speaking in Tongues

We come now in our remaining chapters to the final two potential slogans that we will consider in 1 Corinthians. Each of these is found in the middle of Paul's discussion on community order and the exercise of spiritual gifts, which begins in 12:1 ("Now concerning spiritual gifts") and concludes in 14:40 ("but all things should be done decently and in order"). In this part of his letter, Paul is correcting abuses in public worship. The two possible places where Paul is quoting Corinthians both represent some of the most controversial parts of his correspondence with the Corinthians. As we apply our twelve criteria we will consider if our analysis contributes anything to the longstanding debates surrounding these passages.

Twelve Steps for Identifying Quotations: 1 Cor 14:20–25

"Brothers and sisters, do not be children in your thinking; rather, be infants in evil, but in thinking be adults. 21 In the law it is written, 'By people of strange tongues and by the lips of foreigners I will speak to this people; yet even then they will not listen to me,' says the Lord. 22 Tongues, then, are a sign not for believers but for unbelievers, while prophecy is not for unbelievers but for believers. 23 If, therefore, the whole church comes together and all speak in tongues, and outsiders or unbelievers enter, will they not say that you are out of your mind? 24 But if all prophesy, an unbeliever

The Corinthians and Order

or outsider who enters is reproved by all and called to account by all. 25 After the secrets of the unbeliever's heart are disclosed, that person will bow down before God and worship him, declaring, 'God is really among you.'"

In approaching 1 Cor 14:20–25, three main questions arise: (1) What is the significance of the apparent quote from Isa 28:11–12 in verse 21, particularly given the fact that it does not exactly match either the Masoretic Text (the generally used text of the Hebrew Bible) or the Septuagint (Greek translation of the Hebrew Bible used by most Christians in the first century)? (2) What is the meaning of the term translated "sign" (σημεῖον, *sēmeion*) in verse 22? And (3) How is the assertion in verse 22 connected to the two illustrations in verses 23–25?[1] Most interpreters agree that 14:21–25 is one of the most difficult passages to interpret in all of Paul's epistles. We will briefly survey the more plausible arguments, recognizing that our succinct summaries may not do justice to the complexities of the arguments.

The passage begins with Paul expressing concern that the Corinthians get their thinking on track (14:20). He then cites Isa 28 (14:21), which is followed by an assertion, based on that citation, that tongues are a sign for unbelievers, while prophecy is a sign for believers (14:22). This assertion is in turn followed by two illustrations in the form of conditional clauses (14:23, 24), along with a concluding statement that fleshes out the consequences of the second conditional clause being realized (14:25). The reader would naturally anticipate that the two conditional clauses are provided to support the assertion of the previous verse, if that assertion represents the opinion of the apostle. The problem that scholars have historically noted in 14:21–25 revolves around how the two illustrations in verses 23–24 seem to contradict the assertion of 14:22, rather than confirming it.[2] The assertion of 14:22 states that tongues are meant as a sign for unbelievers and prophecy for believers, but the illustrations that follow depict the negative effect of tongues upon unbelievers (14:23) and the positive effect of prophecy upon unbelievers (14:24–25). How can these apparent contradictions be resolved? The answer may actually be found in acknowledging that Paul is once again quoting Corinthians in 14:22, before refuting their view in 14:23–25.[3]

---

1. Cf. Johanson, "Tongues," 181.

2. Sweet, among others, notes that the illustrations are in fact reversed from what the reader would expect; "A Sign for Unbelievers," 241.

3. Gillespie contends that "there is good reason to suspect that [Paul] here takes up

Among the few scholars who have argued for Corinthian slogans in this passage, some have maintained that both verse 21 and verse 22 represent an extended quotation. Since verse 21 is clearly an Old Testament quote, which both Paul and the Corinthians would embrace as truth, we will not attempt to determine whether Paul is quoting the Corinthians who were themselves quoting Isa 28. What is important is to determine whether or not verse 22 could be a Corinthian statement rather than Paul's own reflection based on Isa 28.

1. *Context: Does the context lead us to expect a quotation?* Yes, potentially. It is critically important that the use of the vocative Ἀδελφοί (*adelfoi*, formally, "brothers") marks what follows as a new subsection. Paul has just made it very clear that although speaking in tongues is great—he does it more than any of the Corinthians (10:18)—ultimately, it has no value for the church without interpretation. Therefore, five words the church can understand are preferable to ten thousand words spoken in a tongue (10:19). Now, in a turn in his argument, Paul exhorts the Corinthians to get their thinking in line with reality. Following the Greek structure more closely, we might translate verse 20: "Brothers and sisters, do not be children in your (way of) thinking; but with respect to evil be infants. In your (way of) thinking be mature!" What is important to notice here is that Paul has just disparagingly referred to how some of the Corinthians were thinking. They were thinking like a bunch of babies! It would not be surprising if Paul were then to cite the infantile thinking with which he is concerned.

There is a second contextual factor that is sometimes overlooked, which may point to a quotation here. Verse 21 clearly introduces an Old Testament quote. That quote, however, does not match any ancient version of the passage that we have. The Hebrew manuscripts upon which our English versions are based essentially reflect what we see in the NRSV: "Truly, with stammering lip and with alien tongue he will speak to this people, to whom he has said, 'This is rest; give rest to the weary; and this is repose'; yet they would not hear" (Isa 28:11–12). Whoever is quoting this passage has placed the words in the mouth of the Lord ("says the Lord," end of 14:22), has changed "he will speak" to "I will speak," has omitted the quote

---

a slogan of the Corinthian pneumatics" (Gillespie, "A Pattern of Prophetic Speech," 81). The following year, Johanson ("Tongues") argued in detail for treating 14:21–22 as Paul quoting Corinthians rather than stating his own opinion.

embedded in Isa 14:12 ("This is rest; give rest to the weary; and this is repose"), and has changed the final part of Isa 14:12 from "yet they would not hear" to "yet even then they will not listen to me." In addition to all of this, they have changed the first part of the quotation so that "strange tongues" is front and center.[4] And after all of these changes,[5] whoever is "quoting" Isaiah feels comfortable adding "says the Lord." The question, of course, is whether this is what the Lord has said at all. The very loose quotation (at best) of this passage may reflect the Corinthians' paraphrase, which was intended to support their contention that is expressed in the 14:22.

2. *Quotative Frame: Is there a "quotative frame" in the near context?* No. While there is a clear quotative frame that introduces the Old Testament quotation in verse 21, there is no formal indication that Paul is quoting someone else as well.

3. *Shift in Person: Is there a shift in grammatical "person"?* No.

4. *Proverbial Statements: Is there a potential slogan in the form of a generalization, like a proverbial statement (usually expressed in the present tense)?* No.

5. *Rhetorical Features: Are there rhetorical features, such as parallel structures, that might suggest an easy to memorize catchphrase?* Yes. Verse 22 has a parallel structure: tongues-not-believers-but-unbelievers; prophecy-not-unbelievers-but-believers. Beyond that, there is a broader rhetorical structure that has typically been overlooked. In 14:20, Paul sets up the structure: "child-thinking, adult-thinking."[6] It may be that he follows that structure in the following verses, with child-thinking being illustrated in verses 21–22 and Paul's corrective adult-thinking being expounded in verses 23–25.[7]

6. *Repetition: Are there expressions that are repeated at other points in the letter?* Yes, perhaps. Paul has earlier stated that "Jews demand signs and Greeks desire wisdom" (1:22). That passage associated unbelieving Jews with signs.

---

4. Cf. the discussion of the differences in Johanson, "Tongues," 181–86.
5. For a helpful summary of the differences, see esp. Garland, 646–47.
6. Cf. Johanson, "Tongues," 186.
7. For more on the highly stylized structure of this passage as a whole, see ibid., 186–90.

7. *Diatribe: Are features of diatribe present or other rhetorical features that may suggest the presence of dialogue between the writer and others?* Yes. Johanson notes the significant parallelism in the rhetoric associated with tongues and prophecy that binds the Isaiah quotation, the assertions, and the illustrations together.[8] Based on his analysis of both the literary and argumentative structure of the text, he concludes that Paul is utilizing common elements of diatribe throughout his argument. We see this, for example, in Paul's citing of a false position in 14:23a, only to refute it with a rhetorical question in 14:23b: "will they not say that you are out of your mind?"

8. *Contradictions: Are there statements that appear to contradict what the author says elsewhere in the same letter?* Yes. Earlier in this chapter, Paul made it clear that tongues are beneficial for believers: "Those who speak in a tongue build up themselves" (14:4), although the "sign" language is not used there. The bigger contradiction is between 14:22 and what follows. As Johanson notes, "While tongues are asserted to be meant as a sign for unbelievers and prophecy for believers [14:22], the illustrations depict the negative effect of tongues on unbelievers and the positive effect of prophecy not on believers but on unbelievers [14:23–25]. The second assertion (*v. 22b*) in particular contradicts the second illustration (*vv. 24–5*) in that it clearly states that 'prophecy is meant as a sign *not for unbelievers* but for believers.'"[9]

9. *Contrast: Does the writer present a sharp contrast or refutation to something he has just stated, which may have been a quotation? Or, does he make a statement and then provide commentary on that statement as if referring to something that has been expressed by others?* Yes. There is a sharp contrast between 14:22 and 14:23–24, with 14:23 effectively refuting 14:22a and 14:24 effectively refuting 14:22b.[10]

10. *Common Issues: Are there expressions that may represent characteristic ways of thinking, based on the broad context of the letter, that the writer appears to be engaging with his audience?* Yes. The Corinthians clearly treated speaking in tongues as a badge of spirituality and also claimed

---

8. Other aspects of diatribe noted by Johanson (ibid., 190) are found in the "abundant use of antithetical parallelism (vv. 20, 22, 23–25), the use of epanastrophe (v. 20), paromoiosis (v. 22), the rhetorical question (v. 23), antistrophy (v. 24), and asyndeton (between vv. 20 and 21 and between the clauses in vv. 24c, d, and 25a)."

9. Ibid., 180.

10. Cf. ibid., 188.

to have special knowledge. When we notice the degree of alterations made to Isa 28:11–12—which we must admit is not beyond Paul doing himself, or could reflect a Greek translation of the passage to which we no longer have access—and the addition of "says the Lord" at the end, we may be dealing with an "insight" that certain Corinthians believe God has given them from this passage, an insight that is then expressed in 14:22.

11–12. *Past Scholars and Common Sense: Is our assessment of a particular putative slogan consistent with the collective wisdom of Bible scholars and Bible translators? Does our assessment of a particular putative slogan pass the common sense test (i.e., does reading a particular text as a slogan or quotation make the best sense of the immediate context)?*

All of our translations indicate that Paul is quoting from the Old Testament in 14:21.[11] None of our translations, on the other hand, use quotation marks in 14:22. This has led readers over the centuries to consistently read 14:22 as Paul's own view of the use of tongues in the assembly, a view that is based on Isa 28:11–12 (quoted in v. 21), but that is then apparently contradicted in the subsequent verses.

When we turn to our commentaries, the consensus is not as strong as the translations. Commentators consistently agree that 14:22 is one of the most difficult verses to interpret in the whole epistle. Hays, for example, believes that the text offers the reader "great confusion," since 14:22 "seems to stand in direct contradiction to the explanation that follows in vv. 23–25."[12] For him, "Paul's argument here is somewhat garbled."[13] Similarly, Fee points to the "notorious difficulties" in this passage.[14] Thirteen of our commentaries appear to read 14:21–22 as Paul's own position despite the apparent contradictions this interpretation entails. This forces interpreters to (1) assume that Paul alters Isa 28:11–12 to meet his rhetorical needs;[15]

---

11. The NJB does not, as a convention, use quotation marks with Old Testament citations.

12. Hays, 239.

13. Ibid., 239–40. Conzelmann (242) simply notes that the tone in verses 21–22 does not agree with the tone found in the rest of the Paul's train of thought, but he does not commit to the possibility that Paul may be quoting the position of the Corinthians in the text.

14. Fee, 677. Cf. Ciampa and Rosner (700), who note that what Paul is saying here is "extremely difficult to unravel."

15. Most commentators recognize that the allusion to Isa 28:11–12 follows neither

and (2) his use of "sign" in 14:22 must be read negatively as a sign of God's judgement (rather than as a positive sign of divine revelation) to make sense of Paul's argument.[16] Garland is representative of most of our commentators when he argues that since unbelievers will not be able to understand the message of tongues, "it assures their unbelief and becomes a sign of God's judgment."[17] These arguments, in our view, rely on the dubious premise that the Corinthians would have interpreted the quotation from Isa 28:11–12 in light of the broader context of Isaiah. It is hard to avoid the conclusion that such an argument would have sailed way over the heads of most (or all!) readers in the church in Corinth.

Not all of our commentators, however, take this view. Fee maintains that "although it cannot be finally proven, the flow of the argument from v. 20, including the strong 'so then' of this sentence, suggests that Paul is setting up this antithesis with the Corinthians' own point of view in mind."[18] Talbert goes further, strongly supporting the presence of a Corinthian

---

the MT nor the LXX fully, often noting Origen's testimony that claims to have found the text of Paul's quote in Aquila's version and other Greek versions that differ from the LXX (see *Philoc.* 9.2). Fee notes that it is possible that Paul and Aquila both depended on an earlier form of Greek text no longer available (*God's Empowering Presence*, 239). Garland (647) points out that the nine differences between 1 Corinthians and the LXX and the MT fits Paul's purposes so well that it seems likely that the reading of the text here "represents an interpretive paraphrase" that Paul adapts for his purposes. Yet, it is also possible that the version of the text being quoted comes from the Corinthian letter that is using this altered version of Isaiah to support their own preference and practice of tongues in the assembly.

16. To make everything "work," scholars tend to rely on the implied context of the Isaiah allusion (unintelligible Assyrian speech). They note that Isaiah is referring to God's judgement on Israel. Since Israel had refused to listen and obey when God spoke through the known language of the prophets, God would bring judgment upon Israel through the conquering Assyrians whose language would be unintelligible. Roberts has noted, however, that although it would be difficult to deny that "the strange-tongued Assyrians were meant to be a sign of judgment to Judah," this does not mean that it is the correct interpretation behind Paul's use of the word "sign" in 1 Cor 14. In fact, if verse 23 is to serve as an illustration related to the quote in verse 21, then it is clear that the two situations are not parallel, since "it is hardly fair to judge and condemn unbelievers on the basis of an unintelligible message uttered by Christians, in the same way that one might condemn unbelieving Judah. The unbelievers as envisaged by Paul hardly seem to be people who have heard the Gospel and spurned it," as Judah had spurned God's prophets (Roberts, "A Sign," 200).

17. Garland, 646; cf. Blomberg, 271.

18. Fee, 681.

quotation in the text.[19] He contends that reading a Corinthian assertion in 14:21–22 followed by a Pauline reply in 14:23–25 not only avoids an obvious contradiction, but also avoids "attributing to Paul a position that is clearly not his."[20] Omanson provides a translation that follows Talbert's argument: "You say that it is written in the Law, 'By men of strange tongues and by the lips of foreigners will I speak to this people, and even then they will not listen to me, says the Lord.' 'Thus,' you claim, 'tongues are a sign not for believers but for unbelievers, while prophecy is not for unbelievers but for believers.'"[21] Read in this way, the Corinthians would be basing their assertion that tongues are a sign not for believers but for unbelievers on their particular understanding of Isa 28:11–12. Paul's response to the false Corinthian assertion would be found in 14:23–25. This analysis has the advantage of passing the common sense test. The apparent contradictions are removed, and Paul's argument flows freely and naturally.

Why, then, do most scholars and virtually no translations embrace this analysis? They essentially reject it based on (1) lack of evidence for a quotation because they have not used explicit criteria for evaluated potential slogans; (2) failing to recognize the importance of 14:20 for setting the structure of what follows; and (3) rightly seeing flaws in earlier arguments for quotations in this passage. We have already spoken to points (1) and (2) above. What remains is to examine the problems with earlier arguments for quotations.

The strongest arguments that Paul is quoting Corinthians here are found in Johanson's important article. Johanson argues that 14:22 should actually be read as a rhetorical question that Paul asks inferentially in light of his quote from Isaiah in 14:21. He maintains that by using the rhetorical question Paul is placing this assertion in the mouth of an imaginary opponent: "Are tongues, then, meant as a sign not for believers but for unbelievers, while prophecy is meant as a sign not for unbelievers but for believers?"[22] Johanson argues that some in Corinth were claiming that

---

19. Talbert, 87. Thiselton (1126) expresses some level of openness to this view, though he ultimately rejects it.

20. Talbert, 87.

21. Omanson, "Acknowledging Paul's Quotations," 212.

22. So also Verbrugge, "1 Corinthians," 383. Johanson ("Tongues," 193) acknowledges that Paul could be quoting an actual slogan cited from Isaiah and made by the Corinthian glossolalists in 14:22 as evidence for their position, or Paul is the one who references Isaiah as a rhetorical argument that he places into the mouth of the diatribal opponent with whom he is conversing.

tongues served as a sign to unbelievers that God was among them. Paul counters this assertion by noting that unbelievers will instead view a bunch of people speaking in tongues as mad.²³

The primary weakness of Johanson's otherwise impressive arguments is the faulty premise on which he bases his argument for a rhetorical question in 14:22: "We already have a clear example of ὥστε [*hōste*] used by Paul to introduce a rhetorical question in Gal. iv. 16"²⁴ He apparently assumes that Gal 4:16 is a clear example based on the fact that most English translations use a rhetorical question here to render the Greek. While a rhetorical question may be one of the best English ways of capturing the *force* of Paul's statement in Gal 4:16, it is highly unlikely that Paul wrote a rhetorical question in Greek. Betz is quick to note that "ὥστε ([*hōste*] 'therefore') introducing a question is odd."²⁵ He refers to Lightfoot, who rightly notes that ὥστε (*hōste*) ought to be followed by a direct assertion rather than a question.²⁶ Moo claims that "the inferential ὥστε [*hōste*] at the beginning of the clause ("and so," "accordingly," cf. Moule 1959:144) is an unusual, though not unprecedented, way of introducing a rhetorical question."²⁷ He goes on to acknowledge that "a few interpreters think that the opening clause may be a statement," before concluding, "but a rhetorical question makes better sense."²⁸ Although it is true that questions can sometimes only be identified

---

23. Johanson ("Tongues," 194) concludes that "Paul is seen to chide the Corinthian glossolalists for their immature thinking in v. 20. Verses 21–5 are to be seen as his argument against this immature thought. The argument is introduced by a quotation of Isa. xxviii. 11–12 with significant alterations in its text. These changes may have either been present already in a Greek translation other than the LXX quoted by Paul or they may have been introduced by Paul himself by way of loose quotation from memory to render the quotation suitable for the purpose in hand. That purpose is to be seen in the use of the text as a springboard for the following assertion in v. 22. These assertions are taken to reflect the content of the glossolalists' childish thought. Paul places them in the mouth of an imaginary opponent as being drawn by inference from the quotation and casts them in the form of a rhetorical question. The opponent is arguing for the authenticating, apologetic sign value of tongues for non-Christians as opposed to Christians, while limiting the same sign value of prophecy to the church. Paul hastens to conclude the argument with his rebuttal in vv. 23–25: tongues would be considered a sign of madness by non-Christians visiting the church at worship, while prophecy would instead by the very thing that would convince the non-Christian visitor."

24. Ibid., 193.
25. Betz, *Galatians*, 228n97.
26. Ibid.
27. Moo, *Galatians*, 286.
28. Ibid., 286n13.

The Corinthians and Order

by the context,[29] what makes sense to a modern reader in a particular passage cannot trump Greek grammar.[30]

Where does this leave us with Johanson's analysis and translation? We have to reject his view that 14:22 represents a rhetorical question.[31] Paul chose to use the conjunction ὥστε (*hōste*, "for this reason," "therefore") to introduce 14:22. This conjunction, when used to introduce an independent clause with an indicative verb, as here, consistently points to a necessary conclusion from what has just been said. The critical question we face, particularly in light of the application of our twelve criteria, is whether the necessary conclusion Paul is introducing is his own or the Corinthians'. We would suggest that it is the Corinthians' conclusion that Paul is citing, which represents the childish thinking he will then refute. If this is correct, then Paul is citing an extended quotation from the Corinthians, which includes both their paraphrase of an Old Testament passage and the conclusion they have reached from the paraphrase (14:21–22). It is thus important to consider whether our supplemental criteria for potential extended quotations will assist us in determining what Paul is doing in this passage.

(1) *Initial Quotative Frame: Is there an initial quotative frame that may introduce an extended quotation?* In this case, we have a clear quotative frame at the beginning of the putative extended quotation: "In the law it is written" (14:21). There is no indication, however, that Paul is going to quote anything other than something from the law.

---

29. See, e.g., John 18:33, where we are told that Pilate said to Jesus, "You are the king of Israel." There are no markers in the Greek text to indicate a question here, but the context makes it clear that Pilate is asking a question rather than stating his opinion.

30. Longenecker nicely sums up the actual grammatical evidence: "Elsewhere in the NT ὥστε (*hōste*, "therefore," "so") is always used at the beginning of independent clauses to draw an inference from what has just been stated (cf. Gal 3:9, 24; 4:7, etc.). Most commentaries acknowledge this. Yet almost all critical texts, translations and commentaries treat v 16 as a rhetorical question" (Longenecker, *Galatians*, 193). He goes on (ibid.) to rightly note, "Nonetheless, linguistically speaking, Burton, Zahn, and Sieffert are right: v 16 must be read as an indignant exclamation that draws an inference from what is stated in vv 14–15 . . . 'So, [it seems,] I have become your enemy because I am telling you the truth!'"

31. If Paul had intended a rhetorical question here, he likely would have framed it in the same way that he framed the series of questions in 12:31, using the negative Greek particle μή (*mē*), which signals to the reader that the question demands a negative answer: "Are not tongues, then, a sign for believers and not unbelievers, while prophecy is not for unbelievers but for believers?"

(2) *Grammatical Extension: Is there grammatical evidence for an extension of the initial quote?* As we have seen above, Paul's use of ὥστε (*hōste*) in 14:22 is most naturally read as him or the Corinthians introducing a necessary conclusion to the statement in 14:21. Thus, the grammar easily allows for 14:22 to be read as an extension of the initial quotation.

(3) *Delayed Response: Is there evidence that Paul's response (commentary or contrast or refutation) might be delayed?* Yes. Paul's use of Ἐὰν οὖν (*ean oun*, "if therefore") to introduce 14:23, along with the content of 14:23 both point to the fact that Paul is here drawing a logical and critical inference from what precedes, expressed in the form of a hypothetical situation. In other words, while verse 23 grammatically fits with the onset of Paul's corrective teaching, verse 22 does not.

(4) *The Writer's Voice: Is there evidence within the putative extended quote that it is the writer's own voice rather than a quotation?* Does the *entire* putative extended quotation make good sense as the words of someone else, or are there portions that strongly appear to reflect the writer's own words? There are no portions of 14:21–22 that clearly must be the words of Paul. Indeed, the apparent contradictions, as we mentioned above, are removed if these verses are read as the words of the Corinthians.

Given the preponderance of evidence we have cited above, we believe that it is quite possible that in this final portion of his argument, which began in 12:1, Paul first tells the Corinthians what he is going to talk about (their current childish thinking and need to have mature thinking, 14:20), and then quotes their letter to him in verses 21–22 to illustrate their childish thinking before setting forth in 14:23–25 what mature thinking would look like. In the Corinthians' letter—remember that this entire section is responding to their letter (see "now concerning" in 12:1)—they first quoted their paraphrase of Isa 28:11–12 and then used it as the foundation for their claim in 14:22 that tongues are an important witness to unbelievers:

> (You wrote,) "In the law it is written, 'By people of strange tongues and by the lips of foreigners I will speak to this people; yet even then they will not listen to me,' says the Lord, thus indicating that tongues are a sign not for believers but for unbelievers, while prophecy is not for unbelievers but for believers!"

The Corinthians and Order

As we noted above, the use of ὥστε (*hōste*) to introduce 14:22 signals that this verse is going to present a necessary conclusion from 14:21. This, in turn, implies that whoever the source of thought is in 14:22 must be the same as the source of thought in 14:21. The fact that these verses, when combined, blatantly contradict what Paul clearly asserts in 14:23–25 strongly suggests that they come from a different source. The fast and loose approach to using the Old Testament represented in 14:21 supports the view that it is not Paul citing Isaiah. On top of this, viewing 14:21–22 as Paul quoting Corinthians and 14:23–25 as Paul's refutation of their position nicely fits with the structure that is introduced in 14:20. With this reading, there are no contradictions in Paul's argument and we need not appeal to a negative meaning for "sign."

The fact that the Corinthians had written Paul for guidance about spiritual gifts (12:1) and the clear indicators that tongues were at the heart of the matter strongly suggest the following reconstruction of Paul's interaction with the Corinthians. Some Corinthians were promoting the practice of speaking in tongues all at the same time during their worship service. This caused chaos and confusion. Not all of the Corinthians embraced this approach to "worship," and so they wrote to Paul for guidance about the use of spiritual gifts among God's people. Those who advocated free expression of the gift of tongues when the church gathered loosely cited the prophet Isaiah in support of this practice, believing that their use of corporate tongues was a sign to unbelievers who were visiting the service. Paul, however, rejects their argument and corrects their flawed thinking and practice in verses 23–25. He makes it clear that instead of creating an atmosphere where visitors will recognize God's presence among them, the chaotic, incomprehensible nature of such a worship service would push unbelievers away in disgust. The Corinthians needed to rethink their perspective on spiritual gifts; they needed to "strive for the greater gifts" (12:31), especially that they might prophecy (14:1).

Likelihood of a Quotation in 14:21–22: *Likely*. Indeed, far more likely than most scholars have recognized in the past.

Theological Implications[32]

So how should this reading of this passage impact the lives of Christ-followers today? To answer this question, we need to first understand Paul's general teaching on the gift of speaking in tongues. Tongues and prophecy are both good gifts when used properly, and neither should be forbidden (14:39); but for the Corinthians, the use of tongues was taking precedence in corporate worship and was actually harming the very purpose for which the gifts were given, i.e., "the building up of the church" (14:12). In the public arena, therefore, prophecy should be the gift for which the body should strive, since it will ultimately, through intelligible conviction, lead the unbeliever to confess God (14:25).[33] While Paul maintains that prophecy is not inherently greater than tongues, since all gifts come from the Spirit and are beneficial for the body (12:7), prophecy is more beneficial for the public assembly because it is intelligible and as a result edifies the entire body (14:5).

While some modern writers have claimed that Paul is essentially condemning tongues in this passage by his use of faint or false praise,[34] in reality, "Paul seeks to regulate tongues, not to eliminate them."[35] He clearly views this spiritual gift as valuable for *individual* worship and prayer (14:4, 18), but he wants his readers to keep a number of things in mind.

First, the gift of tongues is prayer speech, since "those who speak in a tongue do not speak to other people but to God" (14:2, 28). Second, no one understands this prayer speech, since the one praying in tongues is "speaking mysteries in the Spirit" (14:2). Third, the unintelligible Spirit-inspired speech to which Paul refers likely edifies the individual speaking (14:4) precisely because it is a form of "praise" (14:15) and "thanksgiving" (14:17) to God (see also Acts 2:11). Believers are thus edified by carrying out the central purpose of their existence (giving glory to God), even though they do not understand what they are saying. Fourth, Paul insists that he will not refrain from praying and praising in tongues, but insists that believers act in an orderly way by praying/singing with understanding in the public

---

32. See Watson, "A History of Influence" for further discussion.

33. See Talbert's (87–91) excellent literary analysis involving the Corinthian assertion on tongues (14:21–22) followed by Paul's response (14:23–25) and summary (14:26–34).

34. Howe, "The Charismatic Movement," 20–27.

35. Moody, *Spirit of the Living God*, 10.

setting while he encourages praying/singing in the Spirit without interpretation to be done in the appropriate venue of private worship (14:15–19).

Thus, for Paul, praying in tongues is one way that Christians *rightly* pray.[36] What Paul forbids is praying in tongues in the public assembly without interpretation, since it edifies the speaker only and not the entire community (14:28). Congregational utterances in the corporate setting "must be intelligible so that the whole community can be edified. Otherwise, why gather; why not simply pray and sing only in private with no public expression of corporate worship?"[37] This passage, therefore, makes a distinction between appropriate private and public prayer, while maintaining the integrity of "praying in the Spirit" for private worship, where Paul insists he uses tongues more than all of them (14:18).[38] Paul neither forbade tongues, as some modern interpreters contend, nor stood in awe of tongues, as some modern Pentecostals seem to think (along with the Corinthian abusers!). Rather, as with all other forms of Spirit-empowered activity, Paul held tongues in high regard in their proper place.[39] The use of tongues, as with all other spiritual gifts, must promote the building up of Christ's body in unity.[40]

---

36. Fee, *Listening to the Spirit*, 45.
37. Ibid., 46; see also Talbert, 87.
38. Carson, *Showing the Spirit*, 176.
39. Fee, *Listening to the Spirit*, 114.
40. Talbert, "Paul's Understanding of the Holy Spirit," 100.

10

The Corinthians and Order

Women Speaking in Church

For those who love to save the best for last, our final passage will not disappoint. There has been no end of debate surrounding this passage over the past decades, with some scholars even suggesting that Paul did not write the offending portion of it at all. The main issues surround 14:34–35. First, did Paul actually include these verses in his original letter, thus calling for silence among the half of the congregation that was female when God's people gathered together? Second, how should the text be segmented? Was "As in all the churches of the saints" (v. 33b) intended to serve as an introduction to the rest of verse 34 (most versions) or as a supplementary comment connected to verse 33: "For God is not the author of confusion but of peace, as in all the churches of the saints" (NKJV)? Finally, we need to ask: Is it possible that some of the confusion surrounding this passage can be cleared up by recognizing that Paul is once again quoting Corinthians?

Twelve Steps for Identifying Quotations: 1 Cor 14:32–36

"And the spirits of prophets are subject to the prophets, 33 for God is a God not of disorder but of peace. (As in all the churches of the saints, 34 women should be silent in the churches. For they are not permitted to speak, but should be subordinate, as the law also says. 35 If there is anything they desire to know, let them ask their husbands at home. For it is shameful for a woman to speak in

The Corinthians and Order

church. 36 Or did the word of God originate with you? Or are you the only ones it has reached?)"

Before we apply our criteria to determine the relative likelihood of a quotation here, we will first consider the "integrity" of the text. Is the text that we find in our English Bibles what Paul actually wrote? Or, was a portion of it ("women should be silent in the churches") added by later scribes? Those who debate this issue often point to a number of important factors.

First, some Greek manuscripts place verses 34–35 after verse 40. Second, some scholars maintain that if these two verses about the silence of women were totally removed from the text, not only would no violence be done to the argument, but the flow would superficially be improved and the argument would be clearer. These verses seem to interrupt the discussion about speaking in tongues and prophesying to which Paul will return in 14:37–40. Third, verses 34–35 do not seem to fit with the broader context of 1 Cor 12–14, and verse 34 appears to contradict what Paul says earlier (11:5) where he assumes the participation of women in both prayer and prophecy in the Corinthian worship service. Fourth, the appeal to the law in 14:35 appears to be at odds with Paul's practice elsewhere. As a result of such issues, some scholars conclude that these verses were likely placed into the text as a scribal marginal note, possibly derived from Paul's limitation of speech associated with tongues in 14:27–33. Later, as the text was added as a gloss to the manuscript, it began to be perceived as an original inclusion.

These arguments, however, are not as strong as they first appear. First of all, *every* extant Greek manuscript includes verses 34–35. Second, all of the earliest manuscripts include verses 34–35 in their traditional location. Only a few manuscripts have these verses after verse 40, and they are later and less reliable manuscripts. Third, we could identify many places where the removal of particular verses might improve the flow of Paul's argument. Fourth, we need to ask if there are other explanations for the superficial contradiction between these verses and 11:5. Fifth, Paul appeals to the law elsewhere in a positive manner. Contrary to popular modern thinking, he was not anti-law; he was merely against those who attempted to impose adherence to the Mosiac Law on Gentiles as a prerequisite for salvation. Finally, the limitations on the role of women in verses 34–35 have some similarities to those found in 1 Tim 2:11–12. For all of these reasons, and others, we should be very slow to dismiss these verses as not being a legitimate part of the New Testament.

Before we consider whether some of the interpretative problems associated with this text might be solved if we can determine that Paul is quoting Corinthians, we need to first address the second issue mentioned above: How should the text be segmented? In the early Greek manuscripts that we depend on for our New Testament there was no punctuation. In fact, there were not even word breaks, just long strings of capital letters. Thus, when we come to 1 Cor 14:33–34, we are left with two possible ways to segment the passage:

> "And the spirits of prophets are subject to the prophets, 33 for God is a God not of disorder but of peace. *As in all the churches of the saints*, 34 women should be silent in the churches." (NRSV)

> "And the spirits of the prophets are subject to the prophets. 33 For God is not the author of confusion but of peace, *as in all the churches of the saints*. 34 Let your women keep silent in the churches." (NKJV)

Either of these two readings is quite plausible given the Greek original. Both also make good sense in the context. In favor of the latter is the fact that John Chysostom—a native speaker of Greek—and the few scribes that apparently moved verses 34–35 to follow verse 40 all understood verse 33b to go with verse 33a, rather than with verse 34. In order to segment the text in this way, though, Chrysostom took verse 33b to mean "as (I teach) in all the churches of the saints." This suggests that even he had some difficulty in sorting out how this phrase went with verse 33a and, therefore, sought to clarify his thinking for his readers. In the end, it is impossible to conclude with certainty whether verse 33b goes with what follows (NRSV, NIV 1984, NET, ESV, NJB) or with what precedes (NKJV, NASB, NIV 2011, MEV, HCSB). The divergence of opinion reflected in English translations is mirrored in modern commentaries. Eight of the scholars we are considering (Fitzmyer, Keener, Hays, Barrett, Fee, Brookins/Longenecker, Ciampa/Rosner, and Talbert) believe that verse 33b goes with what precedes,[1] while

---

1. Those who take it with what precedes tend to point to the fact that this reading avoids the potentially awkward double occurrence of the word "churches" in the same sentence ("as *in all the churches* of the saints, let women be silent *in the churches*"). In reality, though, it would not be unusual for Paul or any writer to say, "As in all the churches of the saints, let women be silent in the churches (in Corinth)," recognizing that there were likely many house churches in Corinth to which Paul was writing. Advocates of this view, however, also point out that in two other places in this same letter, Paul appeals to a general practice among the churches as a concluding point to his argument (4:17:

The Corinthians and Order

six (Garland, Blomberg, Bruce, Conzelmann, Thiselton, and Witherington) take it with what follows. This is not surprising given the ambiguity in the Greek text.[2]

We will proceed, then, with the assumption that Paul included verses 34–35 in his original letter; but we will leave unanswered the question of whether verse 33b marks the beginning of a new sentence or the end of the preceding sentence. What remains is to consider whether or not Paul is quoting Corinthians in this passage (14:34–35) as, for example, Fitzmyer and Talbert have both argued. We will consider how our criteria apply before examining their arguments for a quotation here.

1. *Context: Does the context lead us to expect a quotation?* No.
2. *Quotative Frame: Is there a "quotative frame" in the near context?* No.
3. *Shift in Person: Is there a shift in grammatical "person"?* No.
4. *Proverbial Statements: Is there a potential slogan in the form of a generalization, like a proverbial statement (usually expressed in the present tense)?* No.
5. *Rhetorical Features: Are there rhetorical features, such as parallel structures, that might suggest an easy to memorize catchphrase?* No.
6. *Repetition: Are there expressions that are repeated at other points in the letter?* No.
7. *Diatribe: Are features of diatribe present or other rhetorical features that may suggest the presence of dialogue between the writer and others?* There are some limited indications of diatribe (rhetorical questions in 14:26 and 14:36).
8. *Contradictions: Are there statements that appear to contradict what the author says elsewhere in the same letter?* Yes. Paul implicitly allows women to speak in 11:5 in the congregation, but commands them to be silent in 14:34.
9. *Contrast: Does the writer present a sharp contrast or refutation to something he has just stated, which may have been a quotation?* Paul

---

"For this reason I sent you Timothy, who is my beloved and faithful child in the Lord, to remind you of my ways in Christ Jesus, *as I teach them everywhere in every church*"; 11:16: "But if anyone is disposed to be contentious—we have no such custom, *nor do the churches of God*").

2. Taylor does not land on a position.

strongly questions the Corinthians' thinking in verse 36, but this would fit regardless of whether what precedes is a quotation or not.

10. *Common Issues: Are there expressions that may represent characteristic ways of thinking, based on the broad context of the letter, that the writer appears to be engaging with his audience?* Yes, but not if these verses were a Corinthian quotation. If verses 34–35 are a Corinthian quotation, the issue would be that the Corinthians were prohibiting women from speaking, and Paul is then correcting that problem. What we have seen thus far in 1 Corinthians, however, is a very strong Corinthian belief in "freedom." Their motto was "all things are lawful for me." So, if verse 34 is a Corinthian slogan, then they are contradicting the very strong "I-can-do-whatever-I-like" attitude that we have consistently seen thus far in the letter, and which appears to be reflected in the immediate context regarding the exercise of spiritual gifts. If, on the other hand, verses 34–35 reflect Paul's words, then Paul is correcting that very attitude once again, this time placing some sort of constraints on women speaking in the assembled church.

11–12. *Past Scholars and Common Sense: Is our assessment of a particular putative slogan consistent with the collective wisdom of Bible scholars and Bible translators? Does our assessment of a particular putative slogan pass the common sense test (i.e., does reading a particular text as a slogan or quotation make the best sense of the immediate context)?* Thus far, the evidence for Paul quoting Corinthians in this passage is not very strong. None of our ten translations treat any portion of verses 34–35 as a quotation. What about our commentators? Most agree with Thiselton's assessment that "translation and exegesis is immensely complex" for this passage.[3] We find essentially three positions in the commentaries under review, with some variations. As we have noted, some maintain that 14:34–35 represents a later addition to the text (an "interpolation"). Hays, Conzelmann, Barrett, and Fee all at least tend to prefer this view. Fee argues that due to the many difficulties associated with textual issues, inconsistencies with what Paul says elsewhere, and interpretative problems associated with the text, that a non-Pauline interpolation is the best option.[4] Similarly,

---

3. Thiselton, 1146.
4. Fee, 705–7.

The Corinthians and Order

Hays also argues that the text is far too general when compared to other parts of the letter:

> Nowhere else in 1 Corinthians does Paul shift in this way to generalized instruction for the churches at large; indeed, this makes no sense at all from a rhetorical point of view in a letter written to a specific congregation, but it does make sense rhetorically if the passage was added at a later time when the letter was being circulated for the guidance of a wider circle of communities.[5]

Conzelmann points to the peculiarities of linguistic usage, interruptions of thoughts, and the secondary fact that some manuscripts read 14:34–35 after what is now 14:40.[6]

Not surprisingly, given the limited evidence the above scholars have been able to marshal, most modern scholars have taken a second view, affirming that Paul wrote 14:34–35. Of the commentaries on which we are focusing, Witherington, Garland, Blomberg, Keener, Ciampa/Rosner, Thiselton, Taylor, and Brookins/Longenecker all reject or appear to reject the interpolation view.[7] These scholars believe that Paul is calling for order and decorum in the Corinthian worship assembly by disallowing the inappropriate behavior practiced by some female believers. Paul's correction is either addressing women who by publicly asking questions of their husbands were disrupting the worship service,[8] women who were interrupting or contradicting their husbands in the context of the public examination or weighing of prophecies,[9] women who were themselves seeking to participate in the public church evaluations about the legitimacy of a given prophecy that was only to be evaluated by church elders (men),[10] or women who were offering questions or speaking in the presence of other men in the assembly, thus causing them to stumble.[11] Thiselton summarizes:

---

5. Hays, 246.
6. Conzelmann, 246. See also Barrett, 330–33.
7. Bruce does not land one way or the other.
8. Witherington, 287.
9. Garland, 673. See also Hurley, "Did Paul Require Veils," 190–220.
10. Blomberg, 281. Yet, see Greenbury, who argues against this view in "1 Corinthians 14:34–35," 721–31.
11. Keener, 118.

> We believe that the speaking in question denotes the activity of sifting or weighing the words of prophets, especially by asking probing questions about the prophet's theology or even the prophet's lifestyle in public. This would become especially sensitive and problematic if wives were cross-examining their husbands about the speech and conduct which supported or undermined the authenticity of a claim to utter a prophetic message, and would readily introduce Paul's allusion to reserving questions of a certain kind for home. The women would in this case (i) be acting as judges over their husbands in public; (ii) risk turning worship into an extended discussion session with perhaps private interests; (iii) militate against the ethics of controlled and restrained speech in the context of which the congregation should be silently listening to God rather than eager to address one another; and (iv) disrupt the sense of respect for the orderliness of God's agency in creation and in the world as against the confusion which preexisted the creative activity of God's Spirit.[12]

In the view of these scholars, to forestall any issues of shame or even misunderstanding, Paul appeals to the church to conduct their meetings in ways that neither dishonor the husband/wife relationship nor detrimentally impact the public order and decency of the community. Keener adds that Paul's prohibition on women does not include Spirit-inspired speech (see 11:5), but only regulates the cultural conflict associated with how women comport themselves in gender-mixed company.[13] Thus, "like tongues-speakers (14:28) and prophets (14:30), women were to remain 'silent' under *some* circumstances."[14]

Finally, Fitzmyer and Talbert both argue that verses 34–35 represent Paul quoting the Corinthians' position from their letter.[15] Fitzmyer believes that these verses represent the position of some Corinthian men who had been actively oppressing women and standing against their participation in the worship assembly. He maintains that Paul's reaction to this oppressive sexist belief is expressed in sharp rhetorical questions in 14:36. In his view, Paul's use of the masculine pronoun μόνους (*monous*, "only ones") in verse

---

12. Thiselton, 1158.
13. Keener, 118.
14. Ibid., emphasis added. Keener notes that Paul's views represent a more progressive voice on gender than many of his day. For a fuller treatment, see Keener, *Paul, Women and Wives*, 70–100.
15. For others who hold this view, see Ciampa and Rosner, 719n203.

36 supports this view.[16] Talbert sees in these verses a second Corinthian assertion in this chapter (the first is 14:21–22), in which Paul quotes the false positions of a Corinthian faction followed by his response (14:36). For Talbert, the text is structured as follows:

Admonition 1: Women should keep silence in the churches

Ground 1: For they are not permitted to speak, but should be subordinate, as the law also says.

Admonition 2: If there is anything they desire to know, let them ask their husbands at home.

Ground 2: For it is shameful for a woman to speak in church.[17]

Talbert argues that theses admonitions reflect the general cultural values from which they originate (e.g., Livy 34:1–8; Juvenal *Satires*, 6; Philo *Hypothetica* 8.7.14; Josephus *Against Apion* 2.201) and run counter to the progressive position taken by Paul elsewhere (e.g., Gal 3:27–28; 1 Cor 11:5; 11:12). Thus for Talbert, since the opinions reflected in 14:34–35 appear to contradict those of the apostle elsewhere, we are forced to the conclusion that this passage reflects either a later interpolation or the position of the Corinthians that Paul is citing.[18] He, with Fitzmyer, opts for the latter solution. In his view, this results in "a coherent, uniformly positive stance of Paul regarding women in the church," which goes against the values of the religious and secular culture of the period.[19]

To sum up, there is clearly no consensus regarding this difficult passage. Eight commentators view the passage as Paul's correction of some Corinthian women who were disrupting the assembly. Five commentators view the passage as material that later scribes added to Paul's letter. And two commentators view the passage as another example of Paul quoting Corinthians in order to refute their faulty thinking. Since the arguments from Talbert and Fitzmyer are limited, we will examine additional arguments that have been put forward for Corinthian quotations in this passage before concluding our analysis.

16. Fitzmyer, 530.
17. Talbert, 91–92. See also the analysis in Allison, "Let the Women Be Silent," 46.
18. Talbert, 92.
19. Ibid., 93.

Quoting Corinthians

We have already seen that Paul almost certainly quotes Corinthians elsewhere in this letter, and he does so repeatedly. We have also seen, in the near context, that these quotations may go beyond brief slogans and include longer segments from a letter the Corinthians sent to Paul (14:21–22). These two factors make the possibility that Paul is quoting Corinthians once again in 14:34–35 at least possible. Several more detailed arguments have been presented for this view, most of which rely to some degree on the efforts of David Odell-Scott. Odell-Scott posits, based on grammatical structure and context, that 14:34–35 likely represents a quotation from a Corinthian faction that asserted "that female silence in worship is expressive of women's subordination to men as dictated by law."[20] He suggests that Paul quotes the position from their letter word for word to "make clear exactly what it is to which he is responding."[21] Odell-Scott maintains that the particle ἤ (*ē*) in 14:36 must be read as a disjunctive particle *used to deny the assertion immediately preceding it*.[22]

Flanagan and Hunter build upon the idea that in 1 Cor 14 Paul is opposing a faction of Corinthian men who insisted upon the subordination of woman.[23] The main impetus for their argument is the masculine form of the word used in 14:36, which is often translated "only ones" (μόνους, *monous*). They argue that if Paul were opposing feminist women, he should be addressing them; but it appears instead that he is addressing men in verse 36. Thus, they argue that the correct translation of 14:36 should be: "What! Did the word of God originate with you, or are you (men) the only ones it has reached?"[24] They posit that 14:34–35, which seems to reflect a traditional Jewish position, must be a quote from the Corinthian letter to which Paul then responds as he has done repeatedly earlier in the let-

---

20. Odell-Scott, "Editorial Dilemma," 69.

21. Ibid.

22. Odell-Scott, "Let the Women Speak," 91. Odell-Scott goes on to note that the same construction exists in 11:20–22, where Paul includes the same particle followed by his rebuttal in the form of rhetorical questions that serve to deny or refute the preceding verses about eating the Lord's Supper in an unworthy manner. Paul states in 11:22: "*What!* Do you not have houses to eat and drink in? *Or* do you despise the church of God and humiliate those who have nothing." Odell-Scott also notes that reading 11:22 as a summation of the preceding verses in 11:20–21 would be absurd, yet that is what many scholars want to do in 1 Cor 14:36 where the same structure is employed (ibid.).

23. Flanagan and Hunter, "Did Paul Put Down Women," 10–12. See also the similar views in Manus, "The Subordination of Women," 183–95; and the more detailed analysis in Allison, "Let the Women Be Silent," 27–60.

24. Flanagan and Hunter, "Did Paul Put Down Women," 11.

ter. And they argue that Paul's chiding of the sexist position in 14:36 is in agreement with Paul's treatment of women elsewhere (1 Cor 11:5 and Gal 3:28), and is much easier to defend than either an anti-feminist rant by Paul or a later interpolation made by a scribe.[25]

Arichea summarizes some of the advantages of reading a Corinthian position/quotation in 14:34–35 followed by Paul's correction:

a) It changes the passage from that of an oppressive text that can be used as an anti-feminist tool to one which advocates the active participation of women within the church.

b) The relationship between 1 Cor 11.5 and 1 Cor 14.34–35 can be more easily explained.

c) It is not necessary to distinguish between the women mentioned in 1 Corinthians 11 and the women mentioned in 1 Corinthians 14.

d) "Speaking" in 14.34–35 and "prophesying" in 11.5 can be taken as referring to the same activity, namely, active participation in the worship service through the proclamation of God's message.

e) The activity referred to in 11.5 need not be different from that which occasioned chapter 14, namely, a regular coming together of the Christian community for worship.

f) The spirit of Gal 3.28 is not violated by Paul in any way.[26]

There are thus a number of significant arguments that have been put forward for the quotation view. Are they sufficient to overturn the preponderance of evidence that we have considered using our criteria, which argues against a quotation here?

We have already seen that neither the grammatical structure nor the context would lead us to expect a quotation here, contrary to Odell-Scott's arguments. And there is no grammatical basis for saying that the particle ἤ (*ē*) in 14:36 has to deny the assertion immediately preceding it. It is clearly disjunctive, in our view, and it clearly denies a Corinthian position; but that does not mean that the preceding verses represent that position. Similarly, the argument that μόνους (*monous*, "only") refers to men because it is masculine gender fails on three counts. First, Koine Greek used masculine gender to refer to mixed-gendered referents. Second, there is no reason

---

25. Ibid., 11–12.
26. Arichea, "The Silence of Women," 110.

to believe that any so-called "feminists" were strictly female. In a church where there were clearly many advocates of an "anything-goes" approach to church life, we would expect both men and women to advocate for open discourse for all when the church gathered to worship. Third, to maintain that reading verses 34–35 as Paul's own view would make those verses represent an anti-feminist rant is to impose modern categories on 1 Corinthians that are utterly foreign to the text and to grossly exaggerate what Paul is communicating. The concern in this passage is clearly not with feminism; it is with church order.

What are we to do with this passage then? Verse 35 actually provides significant guidance. It tells us two things of critical importance. First, the precipitating issue appears to be the desire of some women within the church to learn ("If there is anything they desire to know," v. 35a). Paul's response to this issue likely sheds light on what was happening: "let them ask their husbands at home" (v. 35b). Why does Paul instruct them to restrict their asking to their husbands at home? "For it is shameful for a woman to speak in church" (v. 35c). The language of shame tells us that there is something *cultural* going on in this passage. Ciampa and Rosner cite numerous examples from Greco-Roman texts[27] that are roughly contemporaneous with the New Testament to substantiate the claim made by Christopher Forbes: "There existed in the Graeco-Roman world in our period a strong prejudice against women speaking in public, and especially against their speaking to other women's husbands. In a society with strictly defined gender and social roles, and a strong view of the rights of a man over his wife, such behavior was treated as totally inappropriate."[28]

Paul's concern, then, is with cultural mores of that day, which made open dialogue between women and men in the public sphere inappropriate. Although Paul clearly elevated the place of women elsewhere in his writings—making it clear in 11:5, for example, that women "freely" participated in worship when God's people gathered—he still was not hesitant to restrict any behavior within the church that undermined order, the glory of God, or the edification of the community. His concern in 1 Cor 14 is with speech that undermines that order, whether it be inappropriate speaking in tongues (v. 28), inappropriate prophecy (v. 30), or inappropriate asking of questions (vv. 34–35). Reading verses 34–35 as Paul's words, then, is consistent with the preceding context. There are times when men and

---

27. Ciampa and Rosner, 725–26.
28. Forbes, *Prophecy and Inspired Speech*, 274–75.

women alike are called upon to be silent in the church. Read in this (contextual) manner there is no contradiction between this passage and 11:5; and an apparent contradiction is the strongest argument for a Corinthian quotation here. Indeed, read in this way, none of the arguments that Arichea presents remain an issue. And the limited evidence from our criteria is also addressed. The apparent Contradictions are just that: apparent only. The Contrast in the text is there, but it is between Paul's restrictions and the Corinthians' "anything goes" approach to church life. The latter, in fact, is the Common Issue that Paul addresses in this passage, but that issue is the opposite of what we find in verses 34–35, making a quotation in those verses highly unlikely.

In short, the case against a quotation here is compelling. There are no explicit indicators in the text pointing to a quotation. When this text is compared to likely Corinthian quotations earlier in the letter, this one is much longer and has no quotative frame.[29] There is also no evidence elsewhere in the letter to indicate that the Corinthians held a sexist view. In fact, the letter "suggests the opposite. Paul seeks to curb the Corinthians' unruly and wayward expressions of freedom rather than to encourage them."[30] Hays summarizes the relevant data effectively: "there is no indication in the text that Paul is quoting anything (unlike 7:1) or that the Corinthians held such views about women."[31] Our criteria strongly support Hays's assessment.[32]

Likelihood of a Quotation in 14:34–35: *Unlikely.*

---

29. Although readers might assume we would apply our supplemental criteria in this case, since some scholars posit an extended quotation, the supplemental criteria depend heavily on having a quotative frame at the beginning of the putative extended quotation. No quotative frame is used in this case, leaving the supplemental criteria irrelevant.

30. Garland, 667.

31. Hays, 248.

32. For an interesting debate on the issues in this passage, see Odell-Scott ("Let the Women Speak," 91–93), who argues for a slogan in the text, followed by Murphy-O'Connor ("Interpolations," 81–92), who attempts to refute Odell-Scott and argues for an interpolation in the text, followed again by Odell-Scott ("In Defense," 100–103), where he defends his position further.

Quoting Corinthians

Theological Implications

Since our twelve criteria have led us to conclude that a quotation is unlikely in 14:34–35, we will only briefly consider the theological implications of a quotation in this passage, before turning to the theological implications of reading the passage as Paul's own words. Most of the theological implications for the dubious quotation view have been set forth by Arichea (see above). If Paul is quoting Corinthians in verses 34–35, then he would be firmly rejecting restrictions on women's speech within the assembly. In a context where Paul is highlighting the value of intelligible speech when the church gathers, it would be natural for him to address a related issue from the Corinthians' letter. A certain faction was seeking to enforce the subordination of women and prevent them from participating verbally in the worship assembly. Paul had already *implicitly* acknowledged the right of women to participate verbally in worship in 11:5. Now, he *explicitly* refutes any limitations on women's verbal participation in 14:36. Such a reading would lend significant support to a strong egalitarian approach to ecclesiology today.

As we have seen, however, such an interpretation appears to read modern concerns back into the text and fails to grapple both with the text itself—as our criteria demonstrate—and with what scholars universally affirm about first-century Greco-Roman culture. On the other hand, if one reads verses 34–35 as Paul's own words, then Paul is simply continuing to focus on the issue of order in the worship assembly by emphasizing one more time that control of the tongue is required when God's people gather together. The restrictions Paul imposes are no more anti-woman than his earlier restrictions are anti-tongues (14:28) or anti-prophecy (14:30). The fact that Paul affirms female participation in verbal worship in 11:5 and places restrictions on it here is no more a contradiction than the fact that he says in 1 Thess 5:19 "Do not despise the words of prophets," but restricts the prophets here (14:30). In both cases, he is dealing with different issues in the contrasting passages. In 1 Cor 14, he makes it clear that tongues-speakers are to be silent when there is no interpreter present (14:27–28), prophets are to be silent when other prophets receive revelation (14:29–33), and female inquirers desiring to ask questions are to be silent (14:34–35) for the sake of order in the worship services. In this reading, Paul is not saying that women cannot speak at all in the assembly (see 11:5). Rather, he is addressing a very specific situation that arose given cultural perspectives in the first-century Greco-Roman world. It is not surprising that women may have exercised their newfound freedom to learn alongside their husbands and other men by inadvertently disturbing the orderly flow of worship in Corinth by asking questions during the service.[33] Paul instructs them to ask questions of their husbands when they return home so that the worship service is not disturbed.[34] The question we are left with, then, is how such a reading of the text applies to followers of Jesus today.

Some would simply restrict women from asking any questions in the church service. Given the fact that most churches today do not include a Q & A period, this would have virtually no effect on the life of the church. Alternatively, we might argue that this passage should be applied the same way as Paul's instructions on head coverings in 1 Cor 11. There, the concern was that wives not comport themselves in the worship service in a way that brought dishonor to their "head," i.e., their husband. It is possible that this is Paul's concern here as well. After all, he directs wives to "ask their husbands at home" (v. 35), if they have a question. Paul's concern in 1 Cor 14, however, appears to be more with order than with the husband-wife relationship. So, we would suggest that the most straightforward theological implication would be simply that women should be careful to avoid engaging in theological dialogue when the church gathers in a manner that would disrupt the church. In the first century, this likely meant that women should not speak to males they were not married to in public, which included a church gathering. Since this is not a cultural taboo today, we are perhaps left with the application of women avoiding speech that brings shame to their husband in other ways.

---

33. Keener notes that throughout the first-century world novices (which the newly free women would be) were expected to learn in silence in the public assembly, whereas advanced students were free to ask questions in public lectures (see various passages in Plutarch, *On Listening to Lectures*; Aulus Gellius 18.13.7–8; 20.10.1–6; *Tosefta Sanhendrin* 7:10). Thus, for Keener, in a first-century context, "perhaps the issue was the church's witness in terms of cultural propriety; it was culturally shameful for the women to ask questions" (Keener, "Women in Ministry," 229). Also see Keener, *Paul, Women and Wives*, 139–56.

34. For Keener (*Paul, Women and Wives*, 70), since Paul was addressing uneducated women who were disrupting the service with irrelevant questions, the immediate remedy was for them to stop asking such questions and the long-term solution was to educate the women who for so long had been disenfranchised.

Epilogue

Reading Scripture Responsibly

As we have seen from our brief study of key passages in 1 Corinthians, a number of problems within the church had led to significant divisions, and Paul expends a great deal of energy appealing to members of the congregation(s) in Corinth to become the united body God intended them to be. For that to happen, the whole church had to get on the same theological page and let proper theology drive their behavior. It appears that after Paul left Corinth some within the church began to allow the values of the society around them to increasingly govern both their thinking and behavior.[1] This led to dissension and division, not to mention a host of abhorrent behavior that at times even exceeded the permissive attitudes of the society around them.

Thus, within this one group of Christ-followers we actually find incest being both practiced and tolerated, lawsuits being brought against other church members, apparent openness to visiting prostitutes, an emphasis on individual freedom to the detriment of the welfare of the community, sexual intimacy within marriage being rejected, drunkenness taking place at the celebration of the Lord Supper, and chaos in their worship services. This was a messed up church by any standard! Even with all these difficulties, though, we would be hard pressed to find a Christian community where Paul was more committed to helping them grow and thrive. His intimate relationship with the church is apparent throughout the letter as he responds to what has been reported to him and what has been communicated to him by letter.

---

1. See Winter, *After Paul Left Corinth*.

Paul responds to a range of flawed theological and ethical positions that were being espoused by various groups of Corinthians and were causing serious schisms within the church. And one of the most effective ways that he does so is to first quote certain Corinthians and then refute them. This, we have seen, is in line with common tactics used in ancient Hellenistic rhetoric where philosophers or teachers encountered real or anticipated misunderstandings among their listeners or students. Paul's utilization of this rhetorical device, along with other features of Hellenistic diatribe, is consistent with his writing style elsewhere and provided him with a powerful tool for directly confronting faulty thinking among the Corinthian congregation.

In the past, the debate surrounding possible quotations in 1 Corinthians has often suffered due to a lack of objective criteria for weighing putative quotes. In recent years, a number of scholars have sought to remedy that problem, but none have established and then systematically applied a system of criteria as we have attempted to do above. As we examined ten English translations of the relevant passage, we found that some of the passages are presented as quotations by most of them (1:12; 6:12–13; 7:1; 10:23), others are seldom presented as quotations (8:1; 8:4), and still others are almost never presented as quotations despite that fact that a number of biblical scholars argue that quotations are embedded in the text (6:18; 8:8; 14:21–22; 14:33b–35). Similarly, as we compared major commentaries, we found significant diversity among scholars regarding Paul's use of Corinthian quotations in this letter. In most cases, our criteria have provided support for those who have argued that Paul was quoting Corinthians in particular contexts. And our twelve criteria have also significantly raised the probability of a quotation in 14:21–22. On the other hand, although a number of scholars in recent years have argued that 14:34–35 represent Paul quoting the Corinthians' letter, our criteria strongly suggest otherwise.

Although our study has been limited in its scope, we hope that we have been successful in introducing the issues associated with Paul's possible use of Corinthians slogans in an easy to understand format without oversimplifying complex issues. And while we would agree with Garland's assessment that "interpreters should refrain from resorting to Corinthian slogans or quotations to solve exegetical riddles unless there is clear textual evidence that Paul is citing another's position,"[2] we believe that the application of a clear set of criteria raises the likelihood of frequent Corinthian

2. Garland, 649.

Epilogue

quotations above what some have recognized. Indeed, our analysis suggests that Paul was almost certainly quoting Corinthians in many passages (1:12; 6:12; 6:13; 7:1; 8:1; 8:4; and 10:23), likely quoting them in others (6:18; 8:8; and 14:21–22), and most likely not quoting them in 14:34–35. It is our hope that our analysis will help move scholars toward consensus on the passages we have examined and will serve as a model for students and scholars alike to evaluate potential quotes in other New Testament books.

Beyond that, we hope that the message of 1 Corinthians has been clarified. What Paul has essentially done by quoting Corinthians throughout his letter is to enter into a highly contentious situation by meeting those causing problems on their own turf. He brilliantly uses their own words to drive them toward theological orthodoxy and practical holiness. By quoting Corinthians repeatedly he demonstrates, using their own words, that their thinking and the behavior to which it leads is highly detrimental to their corporate health and growth. He reminds them that despite what individual believers may be "free" to do, what they should be *careful* to do is that which is advantageous to the welfare of the whole community. Plain and simple, the Corinthians needed to adopt a new set of slogans, slogans that rejected the self-seeking, hedonistic trends of the society around them, and instead to recognize that their first priorities as followers of Jesus were now the glory of God and the welfare of the new family to which they now belonged.

Our primary goal in writing this book has been to help readers become more responsible readers of Scripture. We do not subscribe to the myth that we can ever be completely objective in our interpretation of God's Word; but neither do we subscribe to the fatalistic view that we should not even bother to aim for objectivity. First Corinthians was written within a particular cultural, linguistic, historical, and literary context. The more that we can understand that context, the better equipped we will be to approach the text in a manner analogous to how the original readers approached it, and thus the more likely we will be to read the text as they read it. Once we have done that, to the best of our ability, we are ready to ask what the text means for followers of Christ today.

While most scholars acknowledge that Paul included some Corinthian quotations in his letter, many rightfully remain cautious about accepting all of the putative quotations. Many of the relevant passages, especially those found in 1 Cor 8 and 14 continue to present scholars with great interpretive challenges. And whatever the merits of our twelve-step approach presented above, further research remains to be done, particularly given the fact that we are seeking to analyze a single side of a two-sided conversation in 1 Corinthians, and "to some degree any such study will be circular since we determine what was said or written to Paul on the basis of Paul's response; and his response is understood in part on the basis of what was written to him."[3] Despite these limitations, we believe that a systematic application of appropriate criteria can lead to greater confidence when seeking to determine when Paul was quoting Corinthians or members of other congregations in his other letters. And it can also, we hope, lead to what is perhaps Paul's foremost goal in this letter: unity among God's people, whether they are scholars or students.

---

3. Omanson, "Acknowledging Paul's Quotations," 213.

Bibliography

Achtemeier, Paul J., Joel B. Green, and Marianne Meye Thompson. *Introducing the New Testament: Its Literature and Theology.* Grand Rapids: Eerdmans, 2001.

Allison, Robert W. "Let the Women Be Silent in the Churches (1 Cor 14:33b-36): What Did Paul Really Say and What Did it Mean?" *Journal for the Study of the New Testament* 32 (1988) 27-60.

Arichea, Daniel C. "The Silence of Women in the Church: Theology and Translation in 1 Corinthians 14.33b-6." *The Bible Translator* 46 (1995) 101-12.

Aune, David E. *Greco-Roman Literature and the New Testament: Selected Forms and Genres.* Atlanta: Scholars, 1988.

———. *The Westminster Dictionary of New Testament and Early Christian Literature and Rhetoric.* Louisville: Westminster John Knox, 2003.

Barnett, Paul. *The Second Epistle to the Corinthians.* The New International Commentary on the New Testament. Grand Rapids: Eerdmans, 1997.

Barrett, Charles K. *The First Epistle to the Corinthians.* Peabody, MA: Hendrickson, 1968.

Betz, H. D. *Galatians: A Commentary on Paul's Letter to the Churches in Galatia.* Hermeneia. Philadelphia: Fortress, 1979.

Blass, F., and A. Debrunner. *A Greek Grammar of the New Testament and Other Early Christian Literature.* Translated and revised by R. W. Funk. Chicago: University of Chicago Press, 1961.

Blomberg, Craig. *1 Corinthians.* NIV Application Commentary. Grand Rapids: Zondervan, 1995.

Brookins, Timothy A. *Corinthian Wisdom, Stoic Philosophy, and the Ancient Economy.* Society for New Testament Studies Monograph Series 159. Cambridge: Cambridge University Press, 2014.

Brookins, Timothy A., and Bruce W. Longenecker. *1 Corinthians 1-9: A Handbook on the Greek Text.* Baylor Handbook on the Greek New Testament. Waco: Baylor University Press, 2016.

Brown, Raymond E. *An Introduction to the New Testament.* New York: Doubleday, 1997.

Bruce, F. F. *1 and 2 Corinthians.* New Century Bible Commentary. Grand Rapids: Eerdmans, 1971.

Bultmann, Rudolf. *Der Stil der paulinischen Predigt und die kynisch-stoische Diatribe.* Göttingen: Vandenhoeck & Ruprecht, 1910.

Burk, Denny. "Discerning Corinthian Slogans through Paul's Use of the Diatribe in 1 Corinthians 6:12-20." *Bulletin for Biblical Research* 18/1 (2008) 99-121.

Bibliography

Byrne, Brendan. "Sinning against One's Own Body: Paul's Understanding of the Sexual Relationship in 1 Corinthians 6:18." *Catholic Biblical Quarterly* 45 (1983) 608–16.

Caragounis, Chrys C. *The Development of Greek and the New Testament: Morphology, Syntax, Phonology, and Textual Transmission.* Grand Rapids: Baker Academic, 2006.

———. "'Fornication' and 'Concession?' Interpreting 1 Cor. 7:1–7." In *The Corinthian Correspondence*, edited by R. Bieringer, 543–59. Bibliotheca Ephemeridum Theologicarum Lovaniensium. Leuven: Leuven University Press, 1996.

Carson, D. A. *Showing the Spirit: A Theological Exposition of 1 Corinthians 12–14.* Grand Rapids: Baker Academic, 1987.

Carson D. A., and Douglas J. Moo. *An Introduction to the New Testament.* 2nd ed. Grand Rapids: Zondervan, 2005.

Cartlidge, D. "1 Corinthians 7 as a Foundation for the Christian Sex Ethic." *Journal of Religion* 55 (1975) 227–30.

Ciampa, Roy E., and Brian S. Rosner. *The First Letter to the Corinthians.* Pillar New Testament Commentary. Grand Rapids: Eerdmans, 2010.

Conzelmann, Hans. *1 Corinthians: A Commentary on the First Epistle to the Corinthians.* Hermeneia. Philadelphia: Fortress, 1975.

Culy, Martin M. Review of Richard B. Hays, *First Corinthians*; Jerome Murphy-O'Connor, *1 Corinthians*; Allen R. Hunt, *The Inspired Body: Paul, the Corinthians, and Divine Inspiration*; and Rollin A. Ramsaran, *Liberating Words: Paul's Use of Rhetorical Maxims in 1 Corinthians 1–10. Perspectives in Religious Studies* 25 (1998) 394–98.

Dana, H. E., and Julius R. Mantey. *A Manual Grammar of the Greek New Testament.* New York: Macmillan, 1948.

Dodd, Brian J. "Paul's Paradigmatic 'I' and 1 Cor 6.12." *Journal for the Study of the New Testament* 59 (1995) 39–58.

Dooley, Robert A., and Stephen H. Levinsohn. *Analyzing Discourse: A Manual of Basic Concepts.* Dallas: SIL, 2001.

Fee, Gordon D. "1 Corinthians in the NIV." *Journal of the Evangelical Theological Society* 23 (1980) 307–14.

———. *The First Epistle to the Corinthians.* The New International Commentary on the New Testament. Grand Rapids: Eerdmans, 1987.

———. *God's Empowering Presence: The Holy Spirit in the Letters of Paul.* Peabody, MA: Hendrickson, 1994.

———. *Listening to the Spirit in the Text.* Grand Rapids: Eerdmans, 2000.

Fitzmyer, Joseph A. *First Corinthians: A New Translation with Introduction and Commentary.* The Anchor Yale Bible. New Haven, CT: Yale University Press, 2008.

Flanagan, Neal M., and Edwina S. Hunter. "Did Paul Put Down Women in 1 Cor 14:34–36?" *Biblical Theology Bulletin* 11 (1981) 10–12.

Forbes, Christopher. *Prophecy and Inspired Speech in Early Christianity and Its Hellenistic Environment.* WUNT 2.75. Tübingen: Mohr, 1995.

Fotopoulos, John. "Arguments Concerning Food Offered to Idols: Corinthian Quotations and Pauline Refutations in a Rhetorical *Partitio* (1 Corinthians 8:1–9)." *Catholic Biblical Quarterly* 67/4 (2005) 611–31.

———. "The Rhetorical Situation, Arrangement, and Argumentation of 1 Corinthians 8:1–13: Insights into Paul's Instructions on Idol-Food in Greco-Roman Context." *The Greek Orthodox Theological Review* 47/1–4 (2002) 165–98.

Furnish, Victor Paul. *II Corinthians: Translated, with Introduction, Notes, and Commentary.* The Anchor Bible. New York: Doubleday, 1984.

Bibliography

Garland, David E. *1 Corinthians*. Baker Exegetical Commentary on the New Testament. Grand Rapids: Baker Academic, 2003.

———. *2 Corinthians*. New American Commentary. Nashville: B&H, 1999.

Gillespie, Thomas. "A Pattern of Prophetic Speech in First Corinthians." *Journal of Biblical Literature* 97 (1978) 74–95.

Greenbury, James. "1 Corinthians 14:34–35: Evaluation of Prophecy Revisited." *Journal of the Evangelical Theological Society* 51/4 (2008) 721–31.

Hafemann, Scott J. *2 Corinthians*. NIV Application Commentary. Grand Rapids: Zondervan, 2000.

Harris, Murray J. *The Second Epistle to the Corinthians: A Commentary on the Greek Text*. New International Greek Testament Commentary. Grand Rapids: Eerdmans, 2005.

Hays, Richard B. *First Corinthians*. Interpretation. Louisville: John Knox, 1997.

Howe, Claude. "The Charismatic Movement in Southern Baptist Life." *Baptist History and Heritage Society* 13 (1978) 20–27.

Hurd, John C., Jr. *The Origin of 1 Corinthians*. London: SPCK, 1965.

Hurley, James B. "Did Paul Require Veils or the Silence of Women: A Consideration of 1 Cor 11:2-16 and 14:33b-36." *Westminster Theological Journal* 35/2 (1973) 190–220.

———. *Man and Woman in Biblical Perspective*. Grand Rapids: Zondervan, 1981.

Johanson, Bruce C. "Tongues, a Sign for Unbelievers?" *New Testament Studies* 25 (1979) 180–203.

Keener, Craig S. *1–2 Corinthians*. Cambridge: Cambridge University Press, 2005.

———. *Gift Giver: The Holy Spirit for Today*. Grand Rapids: Baker Academic, 2001.

———. *Paul, Women and Wives: Marriage and Women's Ministry in the Letters of Paul*. Peabody, MA: Hendrickson, 1992.

———. "Women in Ministry: Another Egalitarian Perspective." In *Two Views on Women in Ministry*, edited by S. N. Gundry, 205–48. Rev. ed. Grand Rapids: Zondervan, 2005.

Kennedy, George A. *A New History of Classical Rhetoric*. Princeton: Princeton University Press, 1994.

———. *Progynmasmata: Greek Textbooks of Prose Composition and Rhetoric*. Writings from the Greco-Roman World 10. Atlanta: Society of Biblical Literature, 2003.

Kistemaker, Simon J. *Exposition of the Second Epistle to the Corinthians*. New Testament Commentary. Grand Rapids: Baker, 1997.

Klein, William W., Craig L. Blomberg, and Robert L. Hubbard Jr. *Introduction to Biblical Interpretation*. 2nd ed. Nashville: Thomas Nelson, 2003.

Lambrecht, J. "Paul's Reasoning in 1 Corinthians 6,12–20." *Ephemerides Ethologicae Lovanienses* 85/4 (2009) 479–86.

Levinsohn, Stephen H. *Discourse Features of New Testament Greek: A Coursebook on the Information Structure of New Testament Greek*. 2nd ed. Dallas: SIL, 2000.

Longenecker, Richard N. *Galatians*. Word Biblical Commentary. Dallas: Word, 1990.

Mackie, Scott. "The Two Tables of the Law and Paul's Ethical Methodology in 1 Corinthians 6:12–20 and 10:23–11:1." *Catholic Biblical Quarterly* 75/2 (2013) 315–34.

Manus, C. Ukachukwu. "The Subordination of Women in the Church: 1 Cor 14:33b-36 Reconsidered." *Review of African Theology* 8 (1984) 183–95.

Mitchell, Margaret. "Concerning Περὶ δέ in 1 Corinthians." *Novum Testamentum* 31 (1989) 229–56.

———. *Paul and the Rhetoric of Reconciliation: An Exegetical Investigation of the Language and Composition of 1 Corinthians*. Louisville: Westminster John Knox, 1992.

BIBLIOGRAPHY

Moo, Douglas J. "1 Timothy 2:11–15: Meaning and Significance." *Trinity Journal* 1 (1980) 62–83.

———. *Galatians.* Baker Exegetical Commentary on the New Testament. Grand Rapids: Baker, 2013.

———. "The Interpretation of 1 Timothy 2:11–15: A Rejoinder." *Trinity Journal* 2 (1981) 198–222.

Moody, Dale. *Spirit of the Living God: What the Bible Says About the Spirit.* Nashville: Broadman, 1976.

Moule, C. F. D. *An Idiom Book of New Testament Greek.* Cambridge: Cambridge University Press, 1959.

Moulton, J. H., and G. Milligan. *The Vocabulary of the Greek New Testament Illustrated from the Papyri and Other Non-Literary Sources.* Grand Rapids: Eerdmans, 1930.

Murphy-O'Connor, Jerome. *1 Corinthians.* Collegeville, MN: Liturgical, 1979.

———. "Corinthian Slogans in 1 Cor 6:12–20." *Catholic Biblical Quarterly* 40 (1978) 391–96.

———. "Food and Spiritual Gifts in 1 Cor 8:8." *Catholic Biblical Quarterly* 41 (1979) 292–98.

———. "Interpolations in 1 Corinthians." *Catholic Biblical Quarterly* 48 (1996) 81–92.

———. *Keys to First Corinthians: Revisiting the Major Issues.* Oxford: Oxford University Press, 2009.

Nida, Eugene A., and Johannes P. Louw. *Lexical Semantics of the Greek New Testament: A Supplement to the Greek-English Lexicon of the New Testament Based on Semantic Domains.* Society of Biblical Literature Resources for Biblical Study 25. Atlanta: Scholars, 1992.

Odell-Scott, David W. "Editorial Dilemma: The Interpolation of 1 Cor. 14:34–35 in the Western Manuscripts of D, G, and 88." *Biblical Theology Bulletin* 30 (2000) 68–74.

———. "In Defense of an Egalitarian Interpretation: A Reply to Murphy-O'Connor's Critique." *Biblical Theology Bulletin* 17 (1987) 100–103.

———. "Let the Women Speak in Church: An Egalitarian Interpretation of 1 Cor 14:33b–36." *Biblical Theology Bulletin* 13 (1983) 90–93.

Omanson, Roger L. "Acknowledging Paul's Quotations." *The Bible Translator* 43/2 (1992) 201–13.

Porter, Stanley E. "Diatribe." In *Dictionary of New Testament Background*, edited by C. A. Evans and S. E. Porter, 296–98. Downers Grove, IL: InterVarsity, 2001.

Ramsaran, Rollin. A. *Liberating Words: Paul's Use of Rhetorical Maxims in 1 Corinthians 1–10.* Valley Forge, PA: Trinity, 1996.

Richards, Randolph. *Paul and First-Century Letter Writing: Secretaries, Composition and Collection.* Downers Grove, IL: InterVarsity, 2004.

Roberts, P. "A Sign—Christian or Pagan?" *Expository Times* 90 (1979) 199–203.

Robertson, A. T. *A Grammar of the Greek New Testament in the Light of Historical Research.* 4th ed. Nashville: Broadman, 1934.

Runge, Steven E. *Discourse Grammar of the Greek New Testament: A Practical Introduction for Teaching and Exegesis.* Peabody, MA: Hendrickson, 2010.

Schenkeveld, Dirk M. "Diatribe and Dialexis." In *Handbook of Classical Rhetoric in the Hellenistic Period, 330 B.C.—AD. 400*, edited by S. E. Porter, 195–264. Leiden: Brill, 1997.

Siebenmann, Paul. "The Question of Slogans in 1 Corinthians." PhD dissertation, Baylor University, 1997.

BIBLIOGRAPHY

Sim, Margaret G. *Marking Thought and Talk in New Testament Greek: New Light from Linguistics on the Particles ἵνα and ὅτι*. Eugene, OR: Pickwick, 2010.

Smith, Jay E. "The Roots of a 'Libertine' Slogan in 1 Corinthians 6:18." *Journal of Theological Studies* 59 (2008) 63–95.

———. "Slogans in 1 Corinthians." *Bibliotheca Sacra* 167 (2010) 68–88.

Stowers, Stanley Kent. "A 'Debate' over Freedom: 1 Corinthians 6:12–20." In *Christian Teaching: Studies in Honor of LeMoine G. Lewis*, edited by E. Ferguson, 59–71. Abilene: Abilene Christian University Bookstore, 1981.

———. "The Diatribe." In *Greco-Roman Literature and the New Testament: Selected Forms and Genres*, edited by D. E. Aune, 71–83. Atlanta: Scholars, 1988.

———. *The Diatribe and Paul's Letter to the Romans*. Chico, CA: Scholars, 1981.

Sweet, J. P. M. "A Sign for Unbelievers: Paul's Attitude to Glossolalia." *New Testament Studies* 13 (1966–67) 240–57.

Talbert, Charles H. "Paul's Understanding of the Holy Spirit: The Evidence of 1 Corinthians 12–14." *Perspectives in Religious Studies* 11/4 (1984) 95–108.

———. *Reading Corinthians: A Literary and Theological Commentary on 1 and 2 Corinthians*. New York: Crossroad, 1989.

———. *Romans*. Smith and Helwys Bible Commentary. Macon, GA: Smith and Helwys, 2002.

Thiselton, Anthony C. *The First Epistle to the Corinthians: A Commentary on the Greek Text*. New International Greek Testament Commentary. Grand Rapids: Eerdmans, 2000.

Verbrugge, Verlyn. "1 Corinthians." In *Romans–Galatians*, edited by T. Longman and D. E. Garland, 239–414. Expositor's Bible Commentary. Grand Rapids: Zondervan, 2008.

Wallace, Daniel B. *Greek Grammar Beyond the Basics: An Exegetical Syntax of the New Testament*. Grand Rapids: Zondervan, 1996.

Watson, Duane F. "Diatribe." In *Dictionary of Paul and His Letters*, edited by G. F. Hawthorne, R. P. Martin, and D. G. Reid, 213–14. Downers Grove, IL: InterVarsity, 1993.

Watson, Edward W. "A History of Influence: The Charismatic Movement and the SBC." *Criswell Theological Review* 4 (2006) 15–30.

Willis, Wendell. *Idol Meat in Corinth: The Pauline Argument in 1 Corinthians 8 and 10*. Eugene, OR: Wipf & Stock, 2004.

Winter, Bruce W. *After Paul Left Corinth: The Influence of Secular Ethics and Social Change*. Grand Rapids: Eerdmans, 2001.

Witherington, Ben, III. *Conflict and Community in Corinth: A Socio-Rhetorical Commentary on 1 and 2 Corinthians*. Grand Rapids: Eerdmans, 1995.

Author Index

Achtemeier, Paul J., 77
Allison, Robert W., 131, 132
Arichea, Daniel C., 133, 135, 136
Aune, David E., 26, 27, 28, 29
Barnett, Paul, 16
Barrett, Charles K., 9, 43, 44, 52, 55, 65, 75, 88, 92, 96, 126, 128, 129
Blass, F., 34
Blomberg, Craig, 2, 9, 43, 44, 48, 52, 55, 65, 67, 88, 92, 93, 97, 106, 116, 127, 129
Brookins, Timothy A., 9, 43, 44, 52, 55, 65, 90, 91, 92, 95, 96, 126, 129
Brown, Raymond E., 77
Bruce, F. F., 9, 43, 52, 55, 65, 78, 88, 92, 96, 127, 129
Bultmann, Rudolf, 28
Burk, Denny, 7, 24, 25, 30, 35, 60, 61, 62, 64
Byrne, Brendan, 65
Caragounis, Chrys C., 71
Carson, D. A., 77, 123
Cartlidge, D., 78
Ciampa, Roy E., 9, 43, 52, 55, 65, 66, 92, 95, 109, 115, 126, 129, 130, 134
Conzelmann, Hans, 9, 39, 43, 44, 52, 55, 65, 75, 78, 81, 88, 92, 96, 97, 98, 115, 127, 128, 129
Culy, Martin M., xi, 6
Dana, H. E., 34
Debrunner, A., 34
Dodd, Brian J., 7, 65
Dooley, Robert A., 54, 63

Fee, Gordon D., 9, 18, 43, 44, 52, 55, 56, 65, 70, 74, 92, 96, 98, 106, 115, 116, 123, 126, 128
Fitzmyer, Joseph A., 10, 43, 44, 52, 55, 56, 65, 71, 75, 88, 92, 95, 106, 126, 127, 130, 131
Flanagan, Neal M., 132
Forbes, Christopher, 134
Fotopoulos, John, 7, 22, 90, 101
Furnish, Victor Paul, 15, 16
Garland, David E., 10, 16, 43, 44, 45, 51, 55, 65, 71, 76, 78, 79, 81, 88, 92, 96, 113, 116, 127, 129, 135, 140
Gillespie, Thomas, 111, 112
Green, Joel B., 77
Greenbury, James, 129
Hafemann, Scott J., 16
Harris, Murray J., 16
Hays, Richard B., xi, 6, 10, 29, 43, 44, 52, 55, 56, 65, 74, 79, 88, 92, 95, 98, 102, 106, 115, 126, 128, 129, 135
Howe, Claude, 122
Hubbard, Robert L. Jr., 2
Hunter, Edwina S., 132
Hurd, John C. Jr., 5, 17, 19, 31, 39
Hurley, James B., 129
Johanson, Bruce C., 111, 112, 113, 114, 117, 118, 119
Keener, Craig S., 10, 43, 44, 51, 55, 65, 78, 80, 92, 95, 102, 105, 106, 126, 129, 130, 137
Kennedy, George A., 23, 25, 26
Kistemaker, Simon J., 16

Author Index

Klein, William W., 2
Lambrecht, J., 8, 60, 65
Levinsohn, Stephen H., 33, 34, 54, 63, 99
Longenecker, Bruce W., 9, 43, 44, 52, 55, 65, 90, 91, 92, 95, 96, 126, 129
Longenecker, Richard N., 119
Louw, Johannes P., 73
Mackie, Scott, 8, 108
Mantey, Julius R., 34
Manus, C. Ukachukwu, 132
Milligan, G., 33
Mitchell, Margaret, 5, 6, 18, 19, 20, 22, 44, 84, 85, 86, 108
Moo, Douglas J., 77, 118
Moody, Dale, 122
Moule, C. F. D., 118
Moulton, J. H., 33
Murphy-O'Connor, Jerome, xi, 1, 3, 6, 8, 56, 61, 65, 68, 135
Nida, Eugene A., 73
Odell-Scott, David W., 132, 133, 135
Omanson, Roger L., 5, 8, 38, 39, 48, 65, 74, 97, 105, 117, 142
Porter, Stanley E., 28, 30
Ramsaran, Rollin. A., x, xi, 6, 22, 35, 36
Richards, Randolph, 35
Roberts, P., 116
Robertson, A. T., 23, 32, 33, 96
Rosner, Brian S., 9, 43, 52, 55, 65, 66, 92, 95, 109, 115, 126, 129, 130, 134
Runge, Steven E., 41, 54, 63, 90, 99, 100
Schenkeveld, Dirk M., 26, 30
Siebenmann, Paul, 6, 38
Sim, Margaret G., 33
Smith, Jay E., 2, 3, 8, 9, 21, 35, 40, 41, 65, 68
Stowers, Stanley Kent, 26, 27, 28, 29, 30, 61
Sweet, J. P. M., 111
Talbert, Charles H., 10, 43, 52, 55, 56, 65, 78, 79, 81, 82, 88, 92, 93, 95, 98, 106, 107, 116, 117, 122, 123, 126, 127, 130, 131
Thiselton, Anthony C., 10, 18, 43, 52, 55, 58, 65, 67, 73, 76, 78, 86, 92, 95, 98, 108, 117, 127, 128, 129, 130
Thompson, Marianne Meye, 77
Verbrugge, Verlyn, 117
Wallace, Daniel B., 33, 34
Watson, Duane F., 29
Watson, Edward W., x, 122
Willis, Wendell, 35, 88, 92, 98
Winter, Bruce W., 139
Witherington III, Ben, 10, 16, 43, 44, 45, 52, 55, 65, 92, 95, 96, 103, 127, 129

www.ingramcontent.com/pod-product-compliance
Lightning Source LLC
Chambersburg PA
CBHW062004180426
43198CB00036B/2242